HOW TO
APPRECIATE MUSIC

HOW TO
APPRECIATE MUSIC

Sidney Harrison

Elm Tree Books
EMI Music Publishing

Copyright © 1981 by Sidney Harrison

First published in Great Britain 1981
by Elm Tree Books Ltd
Garden House, 57-59 Long Acre, London WC2E 2JZ

in association with

EMI Music Publishing Ltd
138-140 Charing Cross Road, London WC2H 0LD

British Library Cataloguing in Publication Data

Harrison, Sidney
    How to Appreciate Music
    1. Music—Analysis, appreciation
    1. Title
    780'.15   ML63

ISBN 0-241-10681-8
ISBN 0-241-10682-6 Pbk

Printed in Great Britain by
West Central Printing Co. Ltd., Haverhill, Suffolk
Photoset by Premier Metropolis Limited
London E14

Contents

CHAPTER ONE

WHY BOTHER?

There is no best way of listening.

I recall switching on the radio just before a news bulletin I wanted to hear. There was singing. In an instant my wife recognised the singer: I recognised the composer. Who was the better listener?

There are those who 'listen' to music without hearing: they use music to banish silence. There are others who listen not so much to the music as to the performance — for example pianists listening to other pianists' records. There are critics whose thoughts stray from the performance to what they propose to write about it.

Some listeners have a strong bias. The ballet dancer listens, so to speak, with his feet. The folk-song enthusiast hates trained voices. The jazz trumpeter may be deaf to madrigals.

Am I saying that you should be content to listen to whatever takes your fancy, joining the army of people who say 'I know what I like'? No: you begin by knowing what you like and you go on from there. You talk to yourself . . .

I love Schubert's Unfinished Symphony, but with some other symphonies I get lost. I wonder if there are any signposts . . . I wonder if I would like Schubert's *lieder* . . . No I don't think I could sit through a whole evening of songs in German . . . Still, I could get a record of favourite Schubert songs and try one or two at a time. (Later) *Death and the Maiden* is very fine. George tells me that one of Schubert's quartets is called by the same name. He says that the melody of the song is the theme for some variations. I'll ask him what variations are and then borrow his record . . . Last night I saw and heard *La Traviata* on the box . . . I wonder if Aunt Jane would buy me a ticket for the opera for my birthday (what's the difference between an aria and a song?) . . . Half the trouble with me is that I don't know the language. If the programme says Divertimento in D, K205 I don't really know what's meant by Divertimento or 'in D' and, anyway, what's all this K-business? . . . Can I enjoy it without knowing all that? . . . George once persuaded me to go to a Prom when the programme was nothing but avant-garde music. Very strange! But it was somehow nice being there . . . I must really find out . . .

Now read on. If you cannot read music you can ignore the few illustrations. Or maybe you could persuade a friend to play them on the piano.

CHAPTER TWO

THE HEART-BEAT OF MUSIC

Before we wonder how best to listen to an oratorio in a cathedral, an opera in a gilded theatre, jazz on the radio, or a nocturne on your piano at home — and each requires a different pair of ears — let us consider something basic. What is it that propels music? The obvious answer is rhythm — obvious but not simple.

Nature's own rhythm is two-time. We are creatures with two eyes, two ears, two pairs of limbs. We breathe in two-time, our hearts pulsate in two-time, and our lives are governed by night and day, planting and harvesting, departure and return, on and on until the rhythm stops.

Two time, but not exact time. It is only 'dead' matter that vibrates regularly (like the quartz in your watch). Our own rhythm is always, to a lesser or greater degree, irregular. You are right handed or left handed; one of your legs is longer and stronger than the other; your heart never ticks quite like a clock. You may think that a conductor beats time, but in almost every piece of music there are accented and unaccented beats. Occasionally music seems to free itself from the dance of the beats, perhaps in a religious chant, perhaps in operatic *recitativo* — that sung - speech that conveys conversation or explanation. But music without any timing or emphasis would soon become unintelligible.

If I insist on the importance of left-right, down-up, to-fro, you may remind me that a waltz goes in three-time. Quite right! But listen to the bass line: listen maybe to the double-bass in the waltz-band, to the *pizzicato* (plucked) note on the first beat of each bar, and you will hear the to and fro, the back and forth, of two-time.

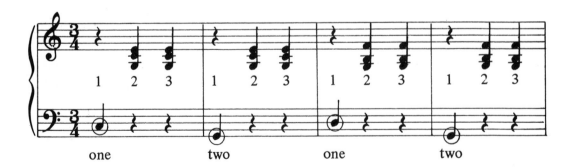

When conducting began to be a recognised speciality, there were elementary books on the subject. No less a person than Berlioz wrote one and drew a diagram to show that two-time is conveyed by a down-beat and an up-beat. A simple notion? Not entirely so. There is a difference between a *down*-up rhythm and an up-*down* rhythm. The up that follows a down beat is not the same as an up that precedes it.

is quite different from:

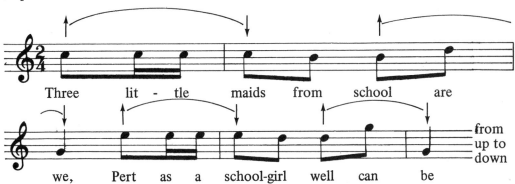

It follows that if there is more than one kind of two-time there will be many varieties of three-time, four-time, six-time and so on.

The Blue Danube, written in quick 3-time, has the feel of slow 4-time, starting on 4th beat and ending on 3rd.

A gavotte in 4-time goes 3-4-/1-2. This gavotte is from Gilbert and Sullivan's *Gondoliers.*

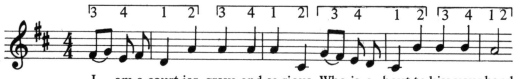

I   am a court-ier, grave and se-rious, Who is a - bout to kiss your hand

6-time, unless at a slow tempo, is felt as 2-in-a-bar.

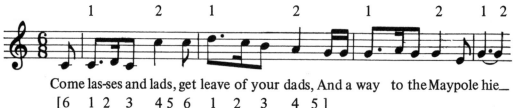

Come las-ses and lads, get leave of your dads, And a way   to the Maypole hie_
[6   1 2   3   4 5 6   1   2   3   4   5]

As an attentive listener you will be surprised to find how many pieces, having begun in a rhythm-pattern, continue with it to the end. And not only in dance music.

At this point we must understand that there are three meanings to the word *beat.* You recognise one of them when you see a conductor's gesture that seems to say 'play *now*.' The now-now-now-now is the pulse of the music, keeping the orchestra in time. The beat, then, indicates a moment.

The conductor, however, may execute a long sweep of the baton. During one such sweep the orchestra may play a complex pattern of notes. Now we can think of a beat not as a moment but as a duration. We are aware of what happens *in* the beat.

The third concept takes us back to the primitive meaning of the word. *Beat* it! This does not necessarily mean a clash of cymbals or a whack on a bass drum. Even in the gentlest melody some notes need to be leant on (even though no accent-signs are in the score); even in a fairy dance there must be some slight taps of emphasis. It is accentuation in all its variety that transforms mere time-keeping into true rhythm.

There is more to all this than *I got rhythm*. But possession of rhythm, the feeling for it, is a fundamental necessity. Academic knowledge of all the complexities of time-values is, of course, admirable, but let us never forget that rhythm existed for centuries before notation was invented. The invention was a stroke of genius. From then on, a musician could put pen to paper and specify whether a sound should last for a beat or two beats or half a beat or whatever. The shape of a note conveyed this information. But the notation of time was based on simple arithmetic, the twice-times table. And *music defies arithmetic.* Only occasionally is it obedient — perhaps in a military march and often in jazz. But how can a performer be arithmetically exact and, at the same time, be passionate, or tragic, or amusing?

When beats are obviously flexible, lingering here, hurrying there, musicians talk of *rubato* (robbed) rhythm. But even the coolest performance of an elegant gavotte must surely not be mechanical. As for an operatic love duet . . . . . .

In *La Bohème,* Puccini instructs Rodolfo (the tenor) to sing 'in a voice full of emotion'.

Your ti -ny hand is fro-zen, let me warm it in - to life

The word *tempo* is sometimes translated as time, and people sometimes talk of quick time and slow time. It is best thought of, however, as speed — the pace of the beats. So one can say of a certain piece that it is in three *time,* that it goes at a slow *tempo,* and that it has the *rhythm* of a *sarabande,* sometimes emphasising not the first beat of the bar but the second.

Amidst all these possibilities, how is one to keep track and recognise 'where the music has got to'? The answer is intuitively known to infants. They clap hands and recite:

1	2	3	4
Ma - ry	had a	lit - tle	lamb, It's
fleece was	white as	snow	(oh); And
ev' - ry -	where that	Ma - ry	went The
lamb was	sure to	go	(oh).

Four fours, and we know that we have come to the end. Even a child knows that *as snow . . . oh* is a half stop, while *to go . . . oh* is a full stop. (Grown-up musicians talk of a half-close or imperfect cadence and then a full-close or perfect cadence.)

You may think that the words indicate the stops. But if we forget the words and say 'Mary had a little lamb, di-*dah* di-*dah* di-*dah*, we still know where the stops occur. And English infants can be taught a French song, perhaps *Sur le pont d'Avignon,* and without understanding a word know where they have got to.

Listening to a complex piece of music, we recognise punctuation: the stopping places, the moments when the music seems to turn a corner with the help of the melodies and harmonies. But listening to rhythm, we are reminded again and again that twice two is four, twice four is eight, twice eight is sixteen. Two-time forms fours, and fours of fours, and fours of eights. How often — how very often — a well remembered section of great music is in exactly thirty-two bars. It forms fours even when the music is in three-time. Do you know Beethoven's famous Minuet in G?

Minuet in G — Beethoven

Four groups of four bars in all. If you obey the repeat-signs (each half played twice) the minuet amounts to 32 bars. This is followed by another section of the same length called the Trio. Then the first minuet is played again, but without repeats.

If you think that a ballroom dance is almost bound to obey arithmetic, turn your attention to opera. That legendary great lover, Don Juan — Mozart's *Don Giovanni* — seduces Zerlina in four-bar phrases (or, rather, attempts to). Again — listen to your favourite symphonies and sonatas, your folk-dances and your ballet music, your hymns and your oratorios, your pop-songs and your *lieder* — you will find an abundance of four-bar phrases.

I first became aware of this when, as a schoolboy, winning Beethoven's sonatas as a prize, I looked at the first one (Op. 2 No. 1) and played the arresting theme, four bars long, and ending with a pause-sign. It seemed to say 'Stop a moment, think of what you've heard . . . and then follow me'.

Listening to heartfelt music, never forget that your physical heart is a pump — to and fro, to and fro . . .

Sometimes, speaking of a moment of excitement, we say 'My heart missed a beat.' Can music miss a beat? Yes, a beat can be conspicuous by its absence. We still feel the beat but there is, so to speak, an accented silence. This is one form of syncopation, and perhaps its best-known usage comes in a sort of musical vulgarism:

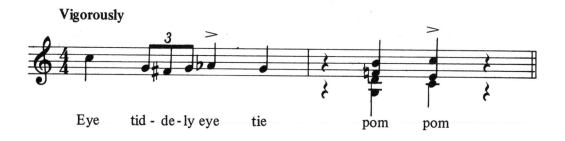

Another kind of syncopation consists of an accent on what is usually an unaccented beat. There is no better example of this than Rossini's *Italian Girl in Algiers* overture. How seldom is a second beat accented in a four-beat bar:

Overture to *The Italian Girl in Algiers* by Rossini
Allegro

ww = woodwind
tutti = everyone,
i.e. full orchestra

To experience yet another kind, count 1 & 2 & 3 & 4 &, and clap your hands on each &.

For any one of these syncopations to be effective, you need a clear normal rhythm against which the syncopated notes can be projected. Sometimes a composer will fail to do this with the result that the syncopated notes are taken to be normal beats by the listener. Schumann often miscalculated in this way. He would start on an &, without a normal beat in the accompaniment, with the result that the 'off-beats' are heard as beats. The audience enjoys what Schumann did not intend.

In the nineteen-twenties and thirties, ballrooms resounded to what was called *syncopated music*, as though syncopation were a new invention. In those pieces the rhythm section of the band maintained a strict beat while a melody instrument or a singer placed the melody notes a bit before or after the beat. Interestingly enough, in a treatise on singing, written round about 1740 in Italy by Pier Francisco Tosi, we find 'In this Place speaking of stealing the Time, it regards particularly the Vocal, or the performance of the Pathetick or Tender; when the Bass goes on exactly regular Pace, the other Part retards or anticipates in a singular Manner.' (I quote from a 1743 translation.)

Is that how Haydn wanted tender melodies to be performed? I make the point that in listening to modern performances one may be permitted to be a little sceptical about classical purity.

Rhythm. Listen to it. Don't ever expect to be able to define it.

CHAPTER THREE

MELODY and HARMONY

God save the Queen (King originally)
(American readers can sing *My Country 'tis of thee*)

God save our gra-cious Queen, Long live our   no-ble Queen, God save the

Why cannot you stop there? Is it because the word *the* needs to go on to *Queen?* No. Even if you sang the tune to *la, la, la,* the F sharp would demand to go to G. Play any major scale, or sing the scale to *doh, ray, me, fah, soh, lah, te, doh'* (you can sing *doh* on any note and go on from there) and you will feel the tug from *te* to top-*doh*. Find your way to a piano and play on the white notes from middle-C to B, and there it is. The seventh note (leading note) is discordant with the first note (tonic or key-note). A discord, by the way, is not a horrible noise. For musicians it is a chord that seems to ask to be 'resolved', and the obvious resolution is on to the concord — the octave, C-C' or, if you want to have a true chord rather than an octave, C E G C'.

Here we arrive at two concepts. One is that going from leading-note to tonic *(te to doh')* whether in the tune or in its supporting chords, often gives us a feeling of arrival — arrival at a cadence — and the other is that discords impart emotional tension to music. As a listener you do not need to apply technical labels to cadences — *perfect* and *imperfect* cadences and so on. But you may well wonder about continuity. If tunes tend to stop on a cadence, how does a long piece go on and on? One method is this: at the moment when your ear expects a perfect cadence, the composer resolves the discord on to another discord. Of all composers, Wagner is the one who most often changes 'The end is nigh' into 'The end is not yet'.

However, Wagner is a relatively late composer, and we must ask where chords came from.

Think of a military bugler. He plays an instrument devoid of mechanism. By means of breath and lip control he is able to produce four different notes. The air in the tube instead of vibrating along its whole length can be persuaded to vibrate in half-lengths, third-lengths, quarter-lengths and so on. And so we arrive at Nature's own chord, consisting of the overtones (sometimes called partials or harmonics) of a fundamental pitch.

14

If you play a note on the piano, you are not normally conscious of overtones. But try this experiment. Find the second-lowest C on the keyboard and push the key down so gently that nothing sounds. The strings of that note are free to vibrate but have not been struck. Hold the note with the left hand and, with the right, play the chord C-E-G in the middle of the keyboard. Play this 'triad' (three note chord) strongly, and immediately snatch your hand away, leaving the left hand still keeping the note C depressed. You will continue to hear the C-E-G chord even though you have taken your right hand away. Where are the sounds coming from? They are coming from the low string which, vibrating in a very complex way, produces the chord, having been persuaded to do so by sympathetic communication from the chord you played. Yes, a low string, suitably nudged by vibrations in the air, can produce a high chord: Nature's chord. The mixture of overtones on any instrument gives colour to the basic sound you consciously hear, and they enable you to know that a note on a trumpet is not like the 'same' note on a clarinet. Never forget the potency of notes you do not consciously hear.

Thinking again of the bugler, we may be pretty sure that in ancient times a shepherd with his pipe (a pipe with holes bored along the side) or a bard with his lyre (a sort of small harp with a few strings of different lengths) must have arrived at something like scales and chords even if their scales and chords were not quite like ours. And if Nero 'fiddled' while Rome burned, you may be sure that an Imperial Band understood something, however simple, about concerted music. Just what it was like we shall never know. Notation was not yet invented, so there are no documents to gladden the eyes of musicologists.

It was not until the eleventh century that notation was invented by a musical monk named Guido d'Arezzo. He drew a ladder of lines (four, not our modern five) and placed notes on or between them. He wrote varying shapes of notes to indicate durations. And he taught his choirboys a Latin hymn in which, if they picked out the first syllable of each line, they found themselves singing a scale — of six notes.* The syllables were *ut re mi fa sol la.* The first syllable of the seventh line did not arrive on the leading note, but this was later inserted and given the syllable *si.* The French still use these syllables. The Italians sing *do* rather than *ut.* (There is no need for you to investigate the evolution of medieval stepwise patterns — the modes — that evolved into our scales; only to know that the evolution explains why some countries use an alphabet from C that goes C D E F G A B C', for their basic 'major' scale.)

---

* *Ut* queant laxis, *Resonare* fibris, *Mira* gestorum, *Famuli* suorum, *Solve* polute, *Labii* reatum, Sancte, Ioannes.

If you want to hear medieval music, you can find records of the music of troubadours and mastersingers, music of courtiers, music of musical merchants and tradesmen, and the simpler music of 'the folk'. You can hear the sounds of their instruments. I refrain from recommending particular recordings since even the most admired performance can be supplanted by something new. To be a serious and perceptive listener you must maintain an interest in reviews of concerts and operas and records and, perhaps, possess a guide to famous records in all catalogues.

However, for most listeners the best starting point is the music of the Renaissance.

During the centuries from the time of Guido onwards, composers were at last able to work like writers and painters — putting down an idea, standing back and looking at it, altering, extending, and combining their thoughts, no longer depending on memory or improvisation. The human voice was available, solo or in choirs, more sensitive and flexible than the early instruments. Composers discovered how to combine high and low voices in complex webs of sound. This was often to the displeasure of both the cardinals and the peasants, but after much controversy a great flowering of 'polyphonic' (many-voiced) music occurred. We follow the melodic lines, enchanted by the way they go in parallel, converge, diverge. Since we do not hear just one tune and accompaniment, or a succession of chords, and since discords were used sparingly, we can easily fail to realise that, if it were possible to stop the flow and listen to what happens at a particular moment, we should undoubtedly hear harmony.

A music student may possess one book on harmony and another on polyphony and counterpoint*, but neither he nor you should regard them as separate activities.

A problem for the listener arises from our tendency to listen to 'the tune', the line we remember, and to take in everything else as just going along with that line. It is easy to persuade yourself, after listening to a record many times, that you know every note of it. But can you sing along with a middle voice or a bass line? I must not make too much of this. As a listener you are not a choir-trainer or a teacher of students of composition. You have the right to sit back and listen to 'the music'. But, just as you cannot take in the architecture of a great cathedral at a glance, you must be prepared not just to listen to a piece but, so to speak, listen *in* it. This process will be easier if, at any time in your life, you have sung in a choir.

*Although polyphony and counterpoint may be similarly defined in the dictionary, we tend in practice to speak of Renaissance polyphony and Baroque counterpoint. See chapter five concerning fugue and its contrapuntal structures.

Nevertheless let us consider chords. We have already spoken of Nature's chord — *doh, me, soh* in tonic-solfa. A child beginner on the piano begins with C-E-G but soon has to learn that, beginning on some other note, he may have to use black keys. He discovers that the white keys may be equidistant physically: not so, aurally.

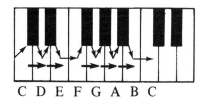

Intervals: Light arrow indicates semi-tone.
Thick arrow indicates tone.

If you want to preserve the proper sequence of tones and semitones, starting on a note other than C, you must learn your scales and the fingering thereof. For one example, E-flat major goes:

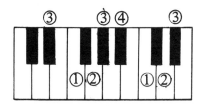

The fingers are numbered 1 to 5, starting with the thumb: ①

Three flats: E♭ A♭ B♭

As a child beginner myself, starting in the key of C, I discovered that Nature's C-E-G could be changed most poignantly by altering E into E-flat. C-E-flat-G is not Nature's chord, but like the musicians of earlier generations I accepted it as a concord and thought it sad. When I was taught the minor scale — E changed into E-flat, and A changed into A-flat — I realised that this would be the source of enjoyable musical tears. I became willing to learn minor scales starting on all possible notes. You will know, of course, that not all pieces permeated by minor harmonies are sad, and you may be aware of the one great funeral march that is in the major key — the Dead March in Handel's *Saul* — but the major-minor, happy-sad, impression is not to be dismissed as mere childishness.

I also enjoyed what is called the chromatic scale, playing all the white and black keys between a note and its octave. What a wealth of lovely discords I was destined to discover! If I encountered a nice 'juicy' chord, I played it all over the keyboard and tried it in other keys. In due course I had to learn, *as I think you should,* the meanings of *transpose* and *modulate,* since transposition and modulation help to make music go ahead, not stopping at the end of a short tune.

Transpose is the easier word. Many an unlettered singer having started on an unsuitable note will turn to his pianist and say 'Put it down a bit' (or up a bit) and you may be aware that *God Save the Queen* is customarily sung beginning on G, while a military band starts on B-flat, a more brilliant key for the brass. But if a composer starts in the key of G can he somehow arrive in B-flat? Oh yes. He must find a suitable chord to effect the *modulation,* and he should choose the right moment to introduce it.

Here is a very simple example. G-major is a one-sharp key, B-flat needs two flats.

G major —
Key of one sharp

G minor —
on the way to . . .

B♭ major —
Key of two flats.

The modulating chord introduces 'foreign' notes into the G-major music. It must not be assumed, however, that *every* foreign note necessarily produces a modulation. it can be a passing chromatic note. Look again at Beethoven's Minuet in G (page 10) and see the sharps in the first phrase that do not produce a change of key.

If a composer begins a movement in G, returns to it from time to time, and ends in it, the movement is 'in G', no matter how many modulations there may be *en route.*

You will find, as you move through musical history, that discords become more and more complex. As a listener you do not need to be able to recognise such chords as a Neapolitan Sixth or a Supertonic Ninth, nor be able to analyse an Enharmonic Change, but you or a friend could try filling up the interval between C and A or A-flat in various ways. (Counting C as *one* this is an interval of a sixth.) Hold each chord for a while and savour it. What an amazing choice there is!

The sixths resolve finally into the major triad.

Thinking of melody and the combined melodic lines of polyphony and counterpoint, thinking of harmony and how it modulates, you may wonder if, as a listener, you need to be 'educated up to classical music'. There is no simple answer to this. Certainly a music lover, perhaps while still a young child, can fall in love with a great piece of music without any tuition. Equally certainly there are 'highly qualified' pundits who know 'all about music' — all about history and criticism and opus numbers — who seem to spend their lives refraining from enjoyment. Some of the great composers had little general education. (It seems that Mozart never went to school since, as a travelling prodigy, he was fully occupied with music.) As song writers they had a feeling for poetry. As opera composers they knew the Greek, Roman, and Biblical stories that were standard subjects. Their tours taught them geography, and their dealings with publishers taught them arithmetic.

But you . . . can you thoroughly enjoy the music of the Renaissance if, having a holiday in Italy, you sit on a beach and can't be bothered to visit Venice or Florence or Rome? Can you enjoy an Elizabethan madrigal, caring nothing for Shakespeare? Have you any thoughts about eighteenth century music of the Baroque era being performed in a twelfth century cathedral to the accompaniment of a nineteenth century organ? Ought you to feel guilty when you enjoy Scarlatti's harpsichord pieces played on the piano?

Pop music may make no demands on the historical sense, but pop music *will* require this if anyone listens to it in a hundred years time.

So, yes, the serious listener needs to be an educated listener, it being understood that self-education is important and that one can disagree with the professors. Never forget that a new crop of professors will almost certainly disagree with our present 'authorities'.

You are fortunate to live at a time when your record-player makes everything available, when records can be borrowed from public libraries, when radio and television bring great performances into your home. If you decide to investigate a kind of music that has not previously interested you, give it time. Whether it is early music or of the *avant garde*, you may come to know it in due course. Here I make what may seem to be a shocking suggestion. Treat it as background music. Have it on while you are cooking a meal or re-painting the spare room. If it begins to grow on you, give it your undivided attention. Do this while you are alone. Talking to your friends (or your enemies) with music in the background is very uncivilised. For me it is quite unbearable.

If, having given a certain kind of music every chance, you fail to enjoy it, by all means say so, but do not deride its admirers. It takes all sorts . . . I would only say: do not imprison yourself in the standard repertoire and do not confine your concert-going to the most expensive artists.

As for 'background', I am not suggesting that you must become an art-historian or be able to write a thesis on the Bourbons, the Romanoffs, and the Hapsburgs. But certain words and expressions should mean something — Reformation, French Revolution, Romantic Movement, Impressionism. If you want to enjoy Verdi's *Otello*, perhaps you should 'brush up your Shakespeare'. If you are an atheist, you should try to understand what Bach 'was on about'. Music is not always self-sufficient. A warning however. A Roman Catholic is not required to admire monastic music; a Scotsman is not required to love the bagpipes; an American is not required to admire ragtime, and you are not required to admire every phrase that Mozart ever wrote.

Accumulate music. As you do so you will probably accumulate books. After all, you are reading this one, are you not?

With this in mind, why not start keeping a list of those pieces which you really enjoyed and would like to hear again? It would also be useful to add some kind of brief description and your personal comments.

Include those items which you found attractive in parts, but perhaps contained passages which were not quite so "easy on the ear": those which you think would be worth another try.

You will find some pages at the end of this book where you can compile your own personal "Listener's Notes".

If your present object is to cultivate and diversify your understanding, let us begin with early music. This may not be the best beginning for a new music-lover, but if you have been a music-lover for a while past it could be a fresh beginning for you.

CHAPTER FOUR

MASSES, MADRIGALS and 'MELODRAMMA' (opera)

When the earth was discovered to be both round and revolving, there was, with almost every revolution, a revolution in ideas: none more shattering than the Protestant Reformation. In some countries out went music sung in Latin; in came hymns sung in German and English and other languages. There was need for a Roman Catholic response. Up till then, the most obviously pious music was monastic chant, Gregorian Chant, a single-line music that avoided the sinful rhythms of the dance and directed the mind to sacred rather than profane love.

Meanwhile the church musicians had been developing polyphonic music for choirs. Some congregations found this too complex, too bewildering. Some churchmen suspected that their choirmasters were more interested in music than in Christianity. Fortunately there was a choirmaster at St. Peter's in Rome who composed a mass for Pope Marcellus that seemed the very model of what polyphonic church music should be. This was Palestrina, and you could do worse than begin your exploration of polyphonic music with his *Missa Papae Marcelli*.

As well as Palestrina, listen to the music of Josquin des Prés, the earliest part-music ever to be printed — in Venice. Seek out the Spaniard, Tomás Luis de Victoria and the Elizabethan Englishman, William Byrd. Do not worry overmuch about such titles as Mass, Motet, Anthem etc., and be sure to hear *Vespro della Beata Vergine* by Claudio Monteverdi. Whatever your religion or philosophy, imagine yourself to be a devout Roman Catholic for as long as the music lasts. Nothing is more important than discovering how to think yourself into a frame of mind. Only a simpleton has one self. Find someone suitable amongst your many selves. After all, in very Catholic Italy there were those who began to be interested in pagan gods.

Strangely, the very kind of music that seemed so very suitable for religious devotion turned out to be adaptable to other purposes.

That great enemy of the Roman church, Martin Luther, wrote 'Is it not singular and admirable that one may sing a simple tune . . . while three, four, or five other voices, singing along, envelop this simple tune with exultation — playing and leaping around . . . as though they were leading a celestial dance, meeting and embracing each other amiably and cordially?'

Such is the music not only of the mass but also of the madrigal. Though some madrigals were religious, we tend to know madrigals as amorous little pieces intended for a very few voices.

In the time of Henry VIII and his daughter the Virgin Queen, the singing of madrigals by people of 'gentle birth' was a much-admired accomplishment. Think of a stately home; a room lit by candle-light; four, eight or twelve voices. The words are mostly amorous, sometimes despairing, in a galant fashion, sometimes triumphant, nearly always from a man's point of view. If the rhythm suggests dancing, and if the words include *with a fa-la-la* or *sing hey nonny no*, do not be surprised if the madrigal is called *Ballett*. There is an extraordinary wealth of English madrigals by William Byrd, Thomas Tallis, Thomas Morley, Orlando Gibbons and others. There are also splendid madrigals by Monteverdi. Madrigals are not crowd-pullers: they are heard at festivals rather than in regular concert series. Fortunately for you, there are admirable recorded anthologies.

Together with madrigals, composers produced beautiful solo songs, some accompanied by those early string instruments called viols, some by virginals (an early kind of harpsichord), yet others by lute. The great lutenist, John Dowland, should be your first choice. His much-admired music was published in eight countries.

The Elizabethan composers wrote solo pieces for the little keyboard instrument variously called a virginal, virginals, or even a pair of virginals (nobody is quite certain why). Such pieces foreshadow what other composers would write for the more developed harpsichord and the still later pianoforte.

One problem we all face is this: we listen to old music with modern ears. We cannot help comparing a viol with a violin, a virginal with a concert-grand piano, a madrigal-group with a choral society. And we may find ourselves listening to madrigals in a too-large, too-bright, too-impersonal concert hall. Fortunately there are groups of singers who, besides singing madrigals, diversify their programmes with other kinds of part-songs including, maybe, some topical items. Madrigals are often regarded as very highbrow, but they can be most persuasive and not at all exclusive.

Remember that you do not have to say 'I like' or 'I don't like'. You can say 'From time to time, I do rather like . . .'

It was part of the creative outburst of the Renaissance that, in the era of the quiet, small-scale madrigal, opera was born — as the result of war.

Greek scholars fleeing to Italy from Islamic armies stimulated interest in ancient classic drama. A coterie of Florentine noblemen — an *accademia* — discussed how the ancient pagan arts, frowned on by the Church, might be revived.

The words were available, the re-nascence of the acting might be possible, but nobody knew, or could know, what ancient Greek music was like. No solution but to compose fresh music, a new music which for us is old and difficult to bring to life. Many manuscripts are lost or exist only in fragments — a top line for the voice, a bass line, a *continuo** above which harmonies might be constructed. For such works the art of 'realisation' must be exercised with a great mixture of scholarship and imagination and, yes, guesswork.

The early works in Florence were called *dramma per musica*. Their successors were called *opera*, nobody knows why. The English word melodrama, with one *m*, declined in dignity, and was applied to simple-minded Victorian plays.

Where shall you begin? If you are already an opera buff beginning to wonder about the pioneer works I can do no better than, once again, refer to Monteverdi and his *Orfeo* or else his *L'Incoronazione di Poppea*. Orpheus is a Greek character: Poppea and Nero appear, very unhistorically, as romantic lovers and are, of course, Roman. The part of Nero was originally written for a high *castrato*, a male singer, who, as a choirboy, was operated on and unmanned to prevent his voice from breaking. Over a long era, well into the nineteenth century, castrati were much admired and highly paid. What shall we do nowadays? Hand the part to a tenor? Dress a woman as a man and let her sing the part?

As you listen to more and more operas be prepared for a multitude of strange conventions. In fairly recent history opera-goers encountered *Der Rosenkavalier* in which a soprano takes the part of a young man who, in a moment of crisis, has to pretend to be a girl! Pay no heed to those who say that operas are absurd. No more so than a Christmas pantomime in which the Principal Boy is a shapely young woman while the Dame is a man. 'The child is father to the man' and you must preserve a certain childlike delight when the lights are lowered and the curtain swings up in the opera house.

To what extent should you interest yourself in scholarship and musicology? Such studies are not essential, but you will gradually become aware of some aspects. For example, Monteverdi was one of the founders of the art that we call orchestration. Ought we then to supply our orchestral players with ancient instruments? What about attempting authenticity? It would be a hazardous enterprise. In the olden days there was no international agreement about pitch. While it is true that viols can be tuned in the minutes before curtain-up, a trumpet made in Venice may find it hard to agree with another made in Naples. International disagreement may have been only slight but problems abound. The much-used phrase 'up to concert pitch' reminds us that agreement on pitch was arrived at only in the era of radio and recording.

* see Glossary

Polyphonic music, whether religious, domestic or theatrical, is not an everday experience for the majority of music-lovers. For some, early music is a late adventure. Indeed for myself it came late. When I was a student, Bach and Handel were the beginning of music proper. Any earlier composers were a specialist-interest. And perhaps for most people early opera is a collectors' item even nowadays.

We shall arrive at standard-repertoire opera in due course. Meanwhile . . .

CHAPTER FIVE

CHURCH AND STATE

'He who pays the piper calls the tune.' When Louis XIV built his great palace at Versailles to which the best people would be invited, he needed skilled servants such as cooks and grooms and gardeners and . . . musicians. He it was who said *L'Etat c'est moi* (*I* am the State). In the years between then and the French Revolution the court heard such great musicians as Lully, Rameau, and a family of musicians named Couperin, the greatest of whom was François. They wrote operas and ballets (of which the common people knew nothing) and they played, and composed for, the *clavecin*, the French harpsichord. Many of the small pieces have the names of court dances (Sarabande, Gavotte, Gigue), names that will recur in the music of Bach, while others have descriptive titles (Little Windmills, Butterflies, The Cuckoo, Sister Monica, Tender Nanette etc.).

Once again I must suggest that you think yourself into the era. You must be a courtier of *l'ancien régime* for as long as the music lasts — never mind if, as a matter of principle, you hate autocracy.

One thing you will observe is that in this French music and in the harpsichord music of Bach and many others, the music is much decorated by what we call ornaments. Was this ornamentation simply an echo of painted ceilings and gilded furniture and elaborate costume? Not entirely. Let us consider the nature of the harpsichord. The basic mechanism is not a felt-covered hammer, hitting a string and bouncing off, as in a piano. It is a jack, a small upright post from which a quill projects. You press down a key, the jack jumps up, and the projecting quill plucks the string. With this you can make very little difference in tone and not much variety of accent. If you insist on variety you had better use a two-manual (two-keyboard) instrument in which an alternative row of jacks possesses not quills but pieces of leather. And you must ask for octave couplers so that, when you play a note, the instrument can obligingly utter that note plus its octave. Even so, you may feel the need to *trill*, setting up a shiver between the printed note and one immediately adjacent to it, or to *turn*, making a sort of walkabout round the note. There is a multitude of signs to indicate these elaborations. Nowadays we argue like mad as to how they should be interpreted or whether some might be omitted when we play harpsichord music on the piano. Is it impermissible to ignore some of the ornaments and instead employ a pianist's variety of touch and accent?

While thinking of the harpsichord we must mention the very small, very quiet clavichord, audible only in a small room. The basic mechanism is not the bounce-off hammer, not the plucking quill, but the so-called tangent that moves up to the string, gives it a little push, and stays in contact until you take your finger away. The tone, quiet though it is, does allow for a little variety. Within limits you can deploy a nice touch. You can produce a crescendo all the way from very soft to soft.

Inevitably there were people in those days who wondered if a keyboard instrument might be devised that would be as brilliant as a harpsichord (not that that had great power) and as responsive to touch as a clavichord. The hammer was the answer, but how could one *fling* it at the strings so that it would bounce off, your finger-energy pushing it only part of the way. How could it escape from its pusher? Escapement was invented in Florence by one Bartolommeo Cristofori in 1709, and he called his instrument the soft-loud — the *piano-forte*. A few people recognised its extraordinary potential, but it remained something of a curiosity until the Germans took it up and developed it. In due course, with the help of Bach's sons and Mozart, it utterly defeated the harpsichord and the clavichord, which remained moribund until revived in this century.

For a long time before this revival, music-lovers simply didn't want to know about harpsichord and clavichord. You, however, may wish to take off your piano-ears and replace them with the ears of Couperin or Scarlatti or Bach or Handel. As you do so, let me warn you that certain titles associated with the piano had different meanings in the era of the harpsichord. The word *sonata* meant something played, as distinct from *cantata*, something sung. Bach composed two-part Inventions but then for his three-part Inventions used the title *Sinfonia*, a word meaning sounding together. *Toccata* (something touched) meant a display of technique rather than a demonstration of what we now call touch. Bach wrote a prelude before each fugue, but a big and grandiose prelude might be renamed *Fantasia*. Beware of simple definitions.

Beware also of the egomaniac pundit who is quite sure that he (or she) alone understands how to play the old music.

If you are in the early stages of cultivating your taste, listening with ever more perceptive ears, turn straightaway to Bach and Handel. Bach was a court and church musician in various German cities and was never well paid. Handel was a famous and usually successful composer and promoter of opera in London. He was a German composing Italian opera for the British aristocracy. Born in the same year as Bach (and Scarlatti) and, inevitably sharing certain characteristics with Bach, he went to Italy and impressed the Italians with his almost immediate command of their sort of music. He then went back to Germany where, for a while, he was employed by the Elector of Hanover. Restless, he went to London, then the richest city in the world, and was soon a court favourite. On the death of Queen Anne, the Elector of Hanover ascended the English throne as George I and was soon reconciled with his former musician.

Handel was nobody's employee. He was a business-like purveyor of Italian opera: his customers the English aristocracy. Some deeply admired him, some formed a cabal against him, and some, grand as they were, thought it perfectly proper to stroll from one box to another in the opera house and carry on their conversations, hushing one-another only when a very expensive Italian was singing an important aria.

What is an aria? It is the expression of powerful thoughts and emotions at an important moment in the drama, much as a soliloquy is an oratorical set-piece in a Shakespeare play, to reveal something to the audience more than to the other characters on stage. It is almost always an example of vocal display. Listening to Handel's arias you become aware that before the aria itself there is a short preliminary *recitativo* (recitative). This is a patter of words, sung in an almost conversational rhythm and provided with only occasional chords for accompaniment. The words set the scene and put you in the picture. Now, whereas a recitative is almost more words than music, an aria is certainly more music than words. The few verbal phrases are repeated again and again, and the natural rhythm of the words gives way to the elaborate rhythms of the vocal line. One syllable may be extended through a long passage in fast notes that demand fine technique and breath-control.

At the end of the first section of the aria there is then some contrasting music, after which the first section is repeated. Though the repeat is indicated by *Da Capo* (from the start again), it was not intended to be a repeat and nothing else. Certainly not! This was the moment when a prima donna departed from the written line, encrusting it with vocal ornaments, elaborating a cadence until it grew into a *cadenza,* convincing the audience that she was worth every guinea of her considerable fee. If, by means of a time-machine, we could hear those performances we might find them 'a bit much'. If Handel's patrons could hear ours, they might find them lacking in taste. A succession of arias does not encourage much stage action or vivid acting, but Handel's audiences were given brilliant spectacle and costume.

The time came when Handel's operatic ventures were no longer successful. He turned to oratorio. *Recitativo* and *Aria* were adaptable, but now there were wonderful choruses; also quartets for the four soloists.

One of these works, *Messiah*, became the most popular, and for most people the most admired, of all religious masterpieces. Each succeeding generation put a new stamp on it. Mozart re-orchestrated it. The Victorians organized monster performances for a thousand voices. It was sung by working-class choirs in provincial non-conformist chapels. *We* try to revive baroque style . . .

Nowadays we cannot help noticing that Handel's music is first choice for grand occasions — *Zadok the Priest* for a coronation, the *Dead March* in 'Saul' for a state funeral. In his own day Handel provided the *'Water Music'* for George I: it was played during a royal procession on the Thames. When George II was celebrating the signing of a peace treaty, Handel provided *Music for the Royal Fireworks.* Even the rehearsal attracted enormous crowds. (In the actual event the fireworks caused a conflagration.)

A Handel organ concerto, a Handel *concerto grosso* — these are enjoyable occasions. What is a concerto grosso? It is a piece in several movements for chamber orchestra. In it there is interplay between a group of select players (the *concertino*) and the orchestra as a whole (the *ripieno*). After Handel's death the word *concerto* began more and more to mean a duet, almost a duel, between a solo performer and orchestra.

Mention of concerti grossi reminds us of the works of this kind that Bach offered to the Elector of Brandenburg (who took no notice). The Brandenburg Concertos are also *concerti grossi,* and they remind us that Bach, a *Kapellmeister,* was provider of music for several princes in succession. A Kapellmeister (spell it with a *c* if you prefer) was chapel-master, the word 'chapel' applying to a music establishment, not to a religious building. Bach wrote great quantities of pleasing music for his patrons. What would our harpsichordists do without the dance-suites full of minuets, gavottes, sarabands, gigues . . . ? How could pianists ignore the toccatas? Why then has his music so often been regarded as very severe?

Unlike Handel, Bach never composed operas, never wrote for the crowds who frequented pleasure gardens and delighted in fireworks. No doubt he had large congregations when he finally settled in St. Thomas's Church in Leipzig, but his listeners were there to hear a long sermon and one of the many cantatas that Bach composed — each being a sacred concert of choruses, ensembles and solo arias lasting perhaps 20 minutes. There are about 200 of these.

Yes, there is a certain severity about Bach's music. When he composed small pieces for his wife (Anna Magdalena's Notebook) and family, there was a suggestion of professional training in the music. And then there were the Two-Part Inventions, quite complex dialogues between right and left hands on the keyboard. There were the Three-Part Inventions that, for some reason, were given the title *Sinfonia.* And what of the 48 preludes and fugues that musicians know under the title of *Das Wohltemperirte Klavier* — The Well-Tempered Keyboard-Instrument? Why so many preludes and fugues? And what does well-tempered mean?

Well-tempered means well-tuned. Are we to understand that the prevailing instruments were ill-tuned? The answer is a qualified 'Yes.'

The fact is that when we sing or play a string instrument, we adjust tuning by ear as we go along. The fixed tuning of a keyboard instrument, however, presents a very peculiar problem. Bach's contemporaries found that if they got the white notes in tune, the black ones never seemed to be quite right. 'Extreme' keys were best avoided (nothing in six sharps, please!). Why was this?

Look at a piano. If you start with the lowest A and then tune the next A, going up octave by octave, you will double the speed of string-vibration with every jump. If the lowest A has x vibrations the others will have 2x, 4x, 8x, 16x etc., until, reaching top-A, you will have multiplied x vibrations by 128. If now you return to bottom A and tune in perfect fifths — A, E, B, F-sharp etc. — you will in due course arrive at the same top A but it will be sharp, for the reason that you are now multiplying the vibrations by 1.5, a process that will arrive not at 128 but at 129.75. This discrepancy was known in ancient times and is called 'the comma of Pythagoras'.

It looks like a very slight fault, but it proved to be a difficult problem. For example, if A-flat were in tune it could not be used as a G-sharp. Nowadays we are so accustomed to those notes being at one pitch that we can hardly believe they were ever conceived of as being different.

Bach advocated, though he did not invent, a way of tuning called equal temperament in which the twelve semitones — C to C-sharp . . . to D . . . to D-sharp and so on — would all be equidistant. In this way *all scales would be equally out of tune* and, for the most part, imperceptibly so. Under this system, your piano tuner makes sure that every fifth is very, very slightly smaller than the 'true' interval. He undergoes a long apprenticeship to 'temper' true tuning. (His other job is to ensure that if three strings are struck by one hammer they will truly be in unison.)

Bach demonstrated the value of equal temperament, with its freedom of the keys, by composing a prelude and fugue in C-major and C-minor, in C-sharp major and C-sharp minor, on and on through the twenty four keys, and he called the collection 'The Well-tempered Klavier'. Later he composed another twenty-four. Hence 'The Forty-Eight', a colossal achievement that has been worshipped by serious musicians ever since.

Equal temperament made possible Bach's richness of harmony and his freedom of the keys. Bach's counterpoint, like, yet unlike, the older polyphony, is full of harmonic progressions that foreshadow Wagner's. They inspired Schumann in the composing of *lieder.*

Since a fugue starts with an unaccompanied theme there seemed to be a need for a prelude. Bach's preludes undoubtedly influenced Chopin's preludes and études. (Chopin practised preludes and fugues before giving a recital of his own music.)

It has to be said that fugues are 'learned' music. Hearing fugues, as a totally new experience, a music-lover might not immediately exclaim 'What lovely pieces!' There seems to be too much going on all at the same time — except for a few, not too ingenious, best-selling examples.

So what is a fugue? It is the supreme example of part-writing. A fugue is composed 'in' three or four voices — occasionally more or fewer — and is developed from an opening, unaccompanied subject (theme). We understand that the word 'voice' may apply to an instrumental line. As for the nature of subjects, they are of extraordinary variety — some only a few notes, others dancing along for quite a while, and in every kind of mood.

For the sake of simplicity let us think of a four-voice fugue in which the parts enter, one after the other, in this order — bass, tenor, alto, treble. We begin, then, with the subject in the bass. At the end of this statement, the tenor voice enters, a fifth higher in pitch. During the tenor entry, the bass continues, singing 'in counterpoint' with it. Soon, not necessarily immediately, the alto voice comes in with the subject, now pitched an octave above the original bass utterance. At this point we have three-part counterpoint. Finally the treble voice, pitched an octave higher than the tenor.

In the order of bass, tenor, alto and treble — piling on top of one another — the entries are easy to follow. But the order could be quite different. You must always 'listen out' to follow the exposition of the fugue.

After the exposition: the development. The subject appears and disappears at one level or another. Sometimes before it ends in one voice it begins in another. There is a device called augmentation that allows every note of the subject to be doubled in duration; also a contrary device called diminution that halves the length of every note. The possibilities are numerous, but it is only rarely that Bach seems to exploit them all. Fortunately for the newcomer in this territory there are some fugues that avoid mind-boggling ingenuity. One such — the *Fantasia and Fugue* in D-minor for organ · became the opening piece in that famous Walt Disney cartoon film called *Fantasia,* played in an orchestral version devised by the late Leopold Stokowski. It made a stunning effect, and the recording became a worldwide best seller. Interestingly, this piece exists in a very effective piano transcription by the great virtuoso, Busoni. Something may be learned about the music — *and about yourself* — by comparing the two transcriptions with Bach's own music, preferably played on a baroque-style organ.

Bach's music submits with remarkable grace to being arranged. This is because it enchants us more by its design than by its colour. His output was enormous. The enquiring music-lover will discover suites for unaccompanied violin, for unaccompanied cello; the double concerto for two violins and orchestra; the *Italian Concerto* without orchestra but designed originally to be played on a harpsichord with two keyboards, and many others that I refrain from cataloguing.

What of Bach played on the piano? It was late in his life when Bach encountered the new and controversial pianoforte. He disliked the first specimen, found some words of praise for an improved model, but never took to it. We have to thank his sons for some of the first piano music. It must be said, however, that there are many pieces by Bach that some of us would rather hear on the piano than on the harpsichord (Philistines that we are!). You must listen to Bach on the harpsichord and decide which pieces you like best on that instrument.

Bach, as we all know, was a great composer of Christian music. It is hard to believe that his oratorio *The Passion according to St. Matthew* lay neglected and un-performed until Mendelssohn as a young man rescued it. Thereafter the Victorians listened to it. They went in great numbers to Bach's *Mass in B-minor.* Nevertheless, most of them preferred *Messiah* . . . and Mendelssohn's *Elijah.*

A word about Bach's chorale preludes. A chorale (*choral* in German, but pronounced with accent on the second syllable) is a hymn. A chorale prelude is a meditation for organ in which the chorale melody appears, disappears, is enveloped in contrapuntal lines. . . . Several of these works have become popular piano pieces.

Unlike Handel, who remained a bachelor, Bach married twice (his first wife died young) and had a numerous family. Three sons are known to fame. Wilhelm Friedemann dissipated his gifts. Carl Philipp Emanuel became a famous Kapellmeister and used the pianoforte to considerable effect. Johann Christian settled in London and was much admired. He was hospitable to a child prodigy named Wolfgang Amadeus Mozart who in after years spoke of him with respect and was certainly influenced by his music.

Are there no other composers of the Bach-Handel period? Oh, yes. As though there were a favourable conjunction of the planets, Bach and Handel shared their year of birth, 1685, with Scarlatti, the composer of around 600 small harpsichord pieces, mostly sparkling and brilliant — delightful in small doses. A slightly older contemporary was Vivaldi (1678) whose copious musical output included some 250 pieces in the Concerto Grosso style. Although best known for his work *The Seasons,* with its extraordinary passages of pictorial writing, since the 1950s his music generally has been enjoying a remarkable revival. There was also Telemann (1681), reputedly the most prolific composer of all time. His prodigious list of works exceeded the combined output of Bach and Handel. Highly renowned during his lifetime, the bulk of his music then lapsed into obscurity only to re-emerge some two centuries later with the renascence of the recorder.

CHAPTER SIX

SYMPHONIES and SONATAS and CHAMBER MUSIC

Every inventor seems to have been anticipated by another, but if anyone can be said to have invented the symphony and sonata-form it was Haydn. However, let us acknowledge Joseph Stamitz whose Mannheim orchestra was the envy of Europe and whose compositions sometimes began with a strong opening theme followed by a more 'feminine' second-subject.

Haydn was the director of music on a very grand estate owned by the very rich and perceptive Prince Esterhazy in Hungary. There he had an orchestra and a great deal of freedom to experiment. What was his problem? It was to write reasonably long works without the help of words or worship or action — how to make music go on without just going on-and-on. The result was a ground-plan that would serve composers for a hundred years. To help you hear your way through a symphony or sonata let me recall once again what happened when, as a child, I won all of Beethoven's sonatas as a prize.

The first movement of the first sonata (Op. 2 No. 1) began with a statement that seemed to say *Listen!* It was short and authoritative, almost demanding to be remembered. After a modulation there were other melodies, several in succession. At the end of page one, there was an end but not *the* end. After all, Beethoven had started in F minor and he couldn't, surely, end in A-flat major. Before turning to page two I was instructed by a special sign to repeat what I afterwards learned was the Exposition. Impatiently I disobeyed. Now page two. It was full of bits and pieces of page one. Treble melodies went over into the bass. Syncopated accents varied the rhythm. . . . This, I afterwards learned, was the Development. Page three began like page one but was not an exact *Recapitulation*. The page-one modulation that had taken the music from F minor to A-flat major was altered so that, when I arrived at *the* end, everything was in the key of the piece.

I had never heard of sonata form or such words as *exposition, development* and *recapitulation*, nor had I ever read the word Ternary. But I got the general idea. Sonatas were composed that way.

As time went on I learned more and more sonatas. My prize volume made me acquainted with Beethoven before either Haydn or Mozart. (Learning music in the wrong order does no harm). I began to realise how adaptable the form could be. Sometimes a Beethoven sonata began with a slow and grand introduction, as in the *Sonata Pathétique* (Op. 13). Sometimes, when the recapitulation was coming to its end, Beethoven would have a number of afterthoughts in a *coda* (tailpiece). In the development he could stay close to his themes or, at other times, almost ignore them. If Haydn or Mozart had lived to hear his later sonatas they would have been very, very surprised, but they would have discerned that their ground-plan was still there. And it has remained there for many later composers.

Growing up I was to discover that sonata form could be found in large-scale symphonies and also in small-scale domestic music — chamber music. Symphonies were for audiences: chamber music was for the pleasure of the players and a few friends assembled in . . . I remembered a phrase from a nursery rhyme — 'upstairs, downstairs, in my lady's chamber.' You, whoever you are, can listen to chamber music, much of which was composed for the well-to-do and the well-educated, because modern affluence and technology have brought the masterpieces to anyone who cares to listen. However, to return to myself when young . . .

From the first movement of that first sonata I turned to the slow movement. Slow? It seemed to be full of quick notes, not only demisemiquavers but occasionally hemidemisemi-quavers (sixty-fourths of a semibreve). How was this? Well, think of a speech equivalent. On a slow beat, clapping hands on each asterisk, say the following:

This   was   a   never-to-be-forgotten moment
  *   *   *   *   *

Seven syllables in a beat. The solution to Beethoven's rhythm was to pretend that each beat was a bar of music, or to count: ONE two three four, TWO two three four, THREE two three four etc. When the time inside a beat was established, it was possible to count according to the long, slow stride of Beethoven's *adagio* *, progressing from time-keeping to heartfelt rhythm: ONE . . . TWO . . . etc.

Sonata-form, which most often applies to first movements, was not necessarily the shape of a slow movement, but I was to discover that 'ternary form' — a thought, diversion, return — was common.

What next? The *Minuet*. In fact, a first minuet, a second minuet, and the first one again, the second minuet being called the Trio. Trio was a puzzling word. Only later did I discover that, some way back in the past, second minuets had been played by only three instruments. The practice died out; the name remained. Minuets went in eight-bar phrases. Of course. Ballroom dances always do.

Minuets were sometimes absent. Some sonatas went: first movement, slow movement, last movement. Some last movements, I found, were called *Rondo*. I enquired about this and was told that in a simple rondo the main tune came back after every departure. In sonata-rondo, however the scheme was: *a b a,* then a

* see Glossary

central *c,* after which a return to *a b a.* As in sonata form the first *a b a* departed from the principal key: the final *a b a* stayed with it.

One more thing: instead of minuet-and-trio there could be a movement that, at first glance, looked much the same but went much, much faster. This was called *scherzo.* The dictionary meaning of the word is joke, and maybe a very fast minuet was originally just that, but a Beethoven scherzo was often no joke. Curiously the middle section was still called trio.

As you listen to scherzi by later composers you may find that a scherzo may come before, not after, a slow movement — for example, in Brahms's second piano concerto. And you will discover pieces called *Scherzo* all on their own — for example the pieces in fast three-time by Chopin, quite divorced from minuet-and-trio form.

I have mentioned the concerto. The concerto with featured soloist (Mozart composed twenty-one piano concerti) is nearly always a box-office attraction. It is designed for virtuosi. It is a show-off piece and, because of the alternation of solo instrument and orchestra, it is very easy to listen to. You will never get lost. Eighteenth century soloists demanded that, somewhere, maybe towards the end of a movement, there should be an opportunity to show off not only technique but improvisation. No doubt some of these improvisations were actually prepared, but they had to have the air of being made up on the impulse of the moment. The name for this sort of display was *cadenza.* The orchestra stopped playing, the soloist took off. How did the orchestra know when to resume? The signal was a trill that ended in a very definite turn that led into the composed music. When composers grew weary of what must often have been tiresome displays and composed their own cadenzas, they maintained the tradition of rhetorical declamation — the style that is called *bravura.* You listen to bravura and you shout 'Bravo!' . . . or are ready to shout bravo when the piece ends. Years ago an audience might shout and clap at the end of a first movement. Not now: it's simply not done. Only in the opera house can shouts interrupt a performance.

Some symphonies have titles. Beware! The London symphonies of Haydn were composed in London. The *London Symphony* of Vaughan Williams is about London.

There are hundreds of works that have something like the form that Haydn evolved — sonatas, symphonies, chamber music, concertos. The amazing fact confronts us that the basic form is endlessly adaptable. Looking through Beethoven's 32 piano sonatas we find sonatas in three or four movements. Three sonatas have only two each. Some movements begin and end abruptly, almost impatiently; some have elaborate introductions and long codas; in some the development of themes is tightly 'argued', while in others Beethoven scarcely bothers. In the Hammerklavier Sonata (Op. 106) the last movement is a long, swirling fugue that seems to be both contrapuntal and rhapsodic. Yet somehow they are all sonatas.

The nine symphonies: how individual each one is! The much loved 'Fifth Symphony' (nobody else's symphony is called The Fifth) has a first movement based almost entirely on four notes — three Gs and an E-flat. The Pastoral Symphony (No. 6) is in part descriptive of a day in the country. The 9th (The Ninth) has a choral last movement that is almost a cantata and is called Ode to Joy. A symphony nevertheless.

You need not be intimidated by the knowledge that Haydn composed more than a hundred symphonies. Many are early works on the way to later and greater ones. Nor are you likely to hear all of Mozart's forty-odd in this genre.

From the time of Beethoven onwards, the works tend to be fewer and longer, the form looser, not so well signposted. Some composers seem a little uncomfortable inside sonata form (think of Chopin's sonatas that are nevertheless magnificent). Others accept it without difficulty (think of Brahms's symphonies, concertos, and chamber music).

The sonata-concept crossed many frontiers. It conquered Tchaikovsky's Russia, Dvořák's Bohemia (Czecho-Slovakia), Sibelius's Finland, and the England of Elgar and Vaughan Williams. It accommodated elements of autobiography, nationality and landscape, and it still allowed us to steer our ears through long movement after long movement. There was a time when the symphonies of Bruckner and Mahler seemed to be almost unendurably long, trying to 'say' almost too much and, in Mahler's so called *Symphony of a Thousand,* calling for immense orchestral and choral resources. Yet they became box-office successes. And what of Shostakovitch and the symphonies that made the Soviet governments wonder just what *he* was trying to say?

At last the climate of opinion among composers changed. Though audiences still loved their symphonies, the new composers were off on a new tack.

Now it is time to think of the meaning of music.

CHAPTER SEVEN

LISTENING TO THE MEANING OF MUSIC

'Go and do your scales' says Mummy. The notes go up and down. With time and effort a C-major scale may become fluently, even gracefully played. You would not expect a child to play an easy major scale with heartfelt emotion. In fact a scale would have to occur as part of a piece of music before it could be played with feeling.

'Now we must learn the minor scale' says teacher. That's different. It is not so much that a minor scale is in itself meaningful but that the difference between the two 'modes' — the contrast — affects the imagination. The child beginner may not realise immediately but will discover later that the contrast may, quite often, be between smiles and tears. (Quite often: not always.)

Where does the sadness reside? Play on the piano — or persuade a friend to play — a melody by Mozart. It won't require great skill. Play the melody more slowly than Mozart intended and listen.

Symphony No. 40 in G minor

Now alter Mozart's notes so that everything is in the major key.

More cheerful, don't you think? If your pianistic skill allows, play both examples a good deal faster, at the tempo, *Allegro molto **, of Mozart's Symphony No. 40. The minor tune is now more buoyant: it almost dances, but is there not still a tinge of sadness, a reminder that life is tragic? How delightful, says one voice. How sad, says another. Is this part of Mozart's magic?

I ask question after question because no-one knows the answer. The music is surely meaningful, but do not, I beg you, try to explain the meaning in words, not even in a poem. When you go to a performance pray that the conductor will not wring too many tears from the music or alternatively try to persuade you that life was too-too charming in the delightful era of rococo art.

Ought you to have a picture in the mind? Well, some people simply cannot prevent themselves from indulging in day-dreaming in the presence of music. This can be dangerous: the dream can obscure the music. But, for my part, I do sometimes imagine Mozart directing a concert, bowing to applause from a duchess and her friends, and saying to himself 'You don't understand the half of it'.

But how is the duchess — or you — to find out? Many works by great composers have no explanatory title and are identified by numbers. We refer to number so-and-so in Book One or Book Two of Bach's Forty-Eight. We are guided by the catalogue of Mozart's works compiled by Ludwig von Köchel and speak of a K-number. We know that Beethoven's first piano sonata is Opus 2, Number 1, and the last is Op. 111. In a few cases Beethoven gives us a title, but *Grosse Sonate für das Hammerklavier* could be regarded as no more than a warning not to attempt such powerful music on the harpsichord. (Beethoven was always searching for bigger and better pianos.)

If a piece acquires a nickname not intended by the composer the public seems always ready to accept it. Beethoven called his Op. 27 No. 2 *Sonata quasi una fantasia* to alert us to the absence of the usual first movement. He begins with a slow movement that seems to anticipate the style of Schubert. A Viennese critic said that the first movement reminded him of moonlight, and *Moonlight Sonata* became and remained the popular title.

Chopin entirely avoided titles of a story-telling kind. What is an *étude*? It is an exploration of a technical problem transformed by Chopin into beautiful music. Of the 27 studies several have acquired nicknames — the *Revolutionary*, the *Winter Wind*, the *Butterfly*, the *Study on black keys*, the *Harp*. On the other hand, Liszt's 'transcendental' studies and concert studies sometimes make us wonder why he called them studies in the first place.

* See Glossary

Seeing the word 'Nocturne' some people mistakenly expect a lullaby and then have to realise that a night-piece can be a passionate invocation to love. And what about all those preludes, by Chopin and others, that are not preludial *to* anything, and all those overtures that, unlike operatic overtures, do not open any proceedings?

Where, then, are we to find clues to meaning? I suggest we think of a title invented by Mendelssohn, who wrote a number of small piano pieces called Songs without Words. Ah yes! If they did have words, what would the words be?

Let us turn back to Bach's Preludes and Fugues. Not only have they no individual titles: most of them have no marks of expression — nothing to indicate fast or slow, loud or soft, grave or gay. Mystified by an *urtext* (source-text) a student can be equally mystified by countless other editions full of would-be helpful(?) metronome speeds, crescendos, staccatos, and, in almost every case, a *rallentando** in the penultimate bar. Fortunately for us, Bach composed a great deal of choral music in which words give us a clue to musical meaning. It is surely sensible to look for resemblances between the music with, and the music without words and to give expression to a prelude or a fugue accordingly.

In music of the romantic era we remind ourselves that Schubert, Schumann, Brahms, Mendelssohn and others were copious song writers. Once again we can find a link between a song and a symphony, piano piece, quartet or whatever. Seeing that most of the songs are about love we can justify the label 'romantic' applied to an immense number of works.

What of music and movement, music and gesture? Music can execute a hop-skip-and-jump, a swoop, a glide. It can stamp, it can plunge, it can twirl. How could there ever be an art of ballet if this were not so? But what a mysterious activity choreography is! In some ballets, movement has dictated the music. Tchaikovsky allowed himself to be told by the choreographer that 32 bars of a certain kind of music would be required at one moment and 16 bars of a different kind at another, and Stravinsky worked closely with Diaghilev's creators of ballet. Nowadays I sometimes see ballets in which I can discern no correspondence between the music and the movements, as though such identity were 'altogether too totally childish, don't you think?'

One thing is certain: the meaning of music in relation to movement is open to many interpretations. When I first heard that a ballet *Armand and Marguerite* would present the story of *La Dame aux Camélias* but not to the music of *La Traviata*† I wondered what music had been chosen. When I learned that it was the Piano Sonata of Liszt (plus a little orchestration but still very much the piano solo) I felt profoundly

*See Glossary
†Verdi's opera was based on 'The Lady with the Camelias' by the younger Dumas. *La Traviata* (The Errant Women) portrayed the romantic and tragic love of a courtesan and a well-bred youth.

sceptical. But the performance wholly convinced me and I could only bow to the genius of Sir Frederick Ashton. It had never previously occurred to me that a sonata with which I was very familiar could be used in this way, nor that its final page could convincingly and movingly accompany a deathbed scene.

Our belief that music has meaning, springs in part from the fact that every instrument in the orchestra has — or can have — a character. Many composers have suggested bird-song with a flute, but do not let us acquire set opinions about the character of an instrument. Debussy began his *L'Après-midi d'un faune* with a flute to suggest not a bird but a goatish, half-human creature playing to the nymphs. Turning to another instrument, you know, of course, that hunting music demands horns, but remember that many a romantic and amorous tune has been uttered by a horn, as in the slow movement of Tchaikovsky's 5th Symphony. A violinist's bow caresses the strings, and the fingers of his left hand convey a shiver, a *vibrato*, to each note. How amorous! But strings can scream through an orchestral storm. The sorceror of Dukas's *The Sorceror's Apprentice* simply has to be a bassoon but please reject the notion that the bassoon is 'the grand-father of the orchestra'.

What about titles as a guide to meaning? Before the time of Bach (and by Bach I mean Johann Sebastian) a great many pieces for harpsichord were given titles. Then there was a change. Bach's contemporary Domenico Scarlatti called his pieces Lessons — they were later called Sonatas.

With the arrival of the all-conquering pianoforte we enter an era of numbered pieces. This is very understandable. How shall one find a title for a sonata in four very different movements — a title that would be equally appropriate for a seemingly tragic slow movement and an obviously light-hearted scherzo? Once in a way Beethoven might give a title — *Sonata Appassionata* or *Sinfonia Eroica* or (applied to one movement only) *Funeral March on the Death of a Hero*, in his Sonata Op.26 — and there is the sonata called *Das Lebewohl* (or *Les Adieux*) where the three movements are labelled respectively, Departure, Absence, and Return. But, like Haydn and Mozart before him, he usually asked his listeners to respond without guidance. Even so, we do know, from conversations remembered by his friends, that his music was, so to speak, inhabited. There were masculine and feminine utterances. And the use of the word *cantabile* (songlike) makes it clear to us that the music was not just music — not, as some people have tried to suggest, 'abstract' music as distinct from 'programme' or descriptive music.

I think we must conclude that any music that is not a mere technical exercise is of flesh and blood.

After the lifetime of Beethoven, the attitude of composers to titles varied a great deal. In the case of Schumann we must inevitably wonder which came first — music or title. Sometimes the answer is obvious. His suite of pieces called *Carnaval* is a picture gallery of characters at a fancy-dress ball. In it we meet traditional characters such as Pierrot, Harlequin, and Columbine. We meet Schumann himself in two different guises (Eusebius and Florestan); also we must play the two pieces called Chopin and Paganini in a style suitable to each of those composers. But in other works there are many pieces that make us suspect an added-on title. Indeed Schumann argued that such a title might enhance a performance. When he composed his *Album for the Young* he knew, as the father of a family, that children enjoy stories and picture-books. So . . . The Merry Peasant, Hunting Song, The Wild Rider. Title first? Title later? We shall never know.

Since music suggests but seldom explains, the composers of the nineteenth century, the Romantic Era, had recourse to a great many almost meaningless titles. Schubert calls some of his smaller pieces *Moment Musical*. Why did he call others *Impromptu*? Brahms called some of his smaller pieces *Intermezzo*. Why did he call others *Capriccio*? Why are his rhapsodies so much less rhapsodic than Liszt's *Hungarian Rhapsodies* (in gypsy style)? What is the difference between Rachmaninoff's *Preludes* and his *Etudes Tableaux*?

When Liszt published several volumes of *Années de Pélerinage* he was inspired by recollections of his early manhood. These reflections on life's pilgrimage are picturesque, almost a pianistic postcard album: here I am beside Lake Wallenstadt, this is me listening to the bells of Geneva, this is Venice, and this was taken after I had been reading Dante. Always him in the foreground . . . and to be played accordingly. But you could never guess the titles from the music. How can Lake Wallenstadt sound different from the Lake of Lucerne?

It was Liszt, taking advantage of the ever improving orchestra, who invented the Symphonic Poem. He was halfway to this concept when he named the three movements of his *'Faust'* Symphony — Faust, Gretchen, and Mephistopheles. But the more loosely constructed Symphonic Poems were even more overtly programme music: *Mazeppa* (after a poem by Victor Hugo), *The Slaughter of the Huns* (after a fresco by Kaulbach) and so on. His greatest successor in this field was to be Richard Strauss with *Don Juan, Don Quixote, Thus spake Zarathustra,* and *A Hero's Life.*

One wonders why Tchaikovsky's *1812* is called Overture rather than Symphonic Poem.

With music of this last type every concert programme, every record-sleeve, tells us what the music is all about. Or does it? Yes, we can hear *La Marseillaise* representing Napoleon's army, we accept the orchestra's tubular bells as representing the real church bells of Moscow, we enjoy the Tsarist national anthem (which, by the way, was not in existence in 1812) but there is music in this such as one cannot find in those Victorian piano pieces called the *Siege of Algiers* or the *Relief of Lucknow*. Even *1812* is not totally explicit.

The meaning of music? Nothing is more mysterious than the persuasive power of music. It means so much, but it never *says*.

This quality of secrecy in a very communicative art (what a paradox!) comes to mind when we listen to chamber music. The very word 'chamber' suggests privacy — shutting out the public. Although we can nowadays buy a ticket for a chamber-music concert, one ought, ideally, to be invited by a cultured host and hostess to join a few friends in their town-house or their country-house to listen to a few musicians. (If you have a decent-sized room, ask a few friends to listen maybe to a student quartet. Pay the students a modest fee and give them food and wine.)

No doubt there are many occasions when a large audience is a welcome sight, but a domestic, intimate situation can be very pleasing. Just one thing may surprise you. When the music is over you may find the players reluctant to talk about the meaning of the music. Amongst themselves they talk about the time of their next journey, the size of their next fee, and the works to be included in their next programme.

CHAPTER EIGHT

SONG

If there is one kind of music you don't need to be 'educated up to', it is what one might call the ordinary song. Songs were invented and sung long before there was formal education. Illiterate peasants invented folk-songs, uneducated sailors invented sea-shanties, black slaves invented spirituals. Most of our pop singers 'write' songs that they cannot read. And let us not forget that witty, sophisticated Noel Coward never *wrote* a song. He invented it at the piano. An amanuensis put it on paper, and an orchestrator arranged it for a show. Almost every kind of song — music-hall ditty or smooth drawing-room ballad — is quickly assimilable.

There is, however, a special category, the *lieder* recital. The German word *lied*, by the way, means song. *Lieder* is the plural form. So perhaps we ought to say Songs Recital. This trivial point is worth making because we must ask if *lieder* are translatable.

Though a *lieder* recital may include something by Mozart and Beethoven, the starting point is generally Schubert. He was born at a time of revolution and war amidst a swiftly changing environment. In manhood he was deeply influenced by a new lyric-romantic poetry full of personal anguish, ecstasy, introspection, laughter-and-tears. And there was the ever improving pianoforte - improving largely because Beethoven's music had demanded bigger and better and stronger pianos. Thousands of people were buying pianos. A piano in the home began to seem almost as necessary as a fireplace. No doubt a great deal of rubbish was played on domestic pianos, but there were musical families who played and sang and invited their friends for chamber music.

When people refer to Schubert as perhaps the greatest of song writers, I like to make the point that he created a new kind of accompaniment, to be emulated by Schumann, Brahms, and others. Few aspects of music are more mysterious than the affinity between the piano, with its hammers bouncing off steel strings, and the voice energised by the breath of life and emotion. In some *lieder* accompaniments there is some slight element of descriptiveness, perhaps 'rippling' semiquavers in a song about a streamlet beside which an unhappy young man wanders. But there is no actual resemblance between piano sounds and water sounds. When in *The Erl-King* Schubert makes us think of a galloping horse he does it by means of a rhythm in triplets. Triplets for a four-legged animal! We accept it: we know nothing could be more right . . . true genius from a teenage composer.

At this point you may ask whether singer and pianist are an equal partnership. No: not quite. You buy a ticket to hear a fine singer, not to hear a fine accompanist, though you may hope that the piano will be sensitively played. It is the singer who faces the audience, whose face mirrors the emotions. The accompanist must adopt the singer's ideas, playing a little differently for every different singer. Of course the pianist's mind and fingers are of incalculable importance, but years after a great recital you may say 'I once heard so-and-so sing that marvellously. The accompanist? I can't quite remember. Probably such-and-such: it was usually him.'

A piano-and-violin recital is different. I have myself argued often enough with a violinist partner. I have not argued with a singer unless he wants to do something that would compel me to play badly.

However, at a *lieder* recital you should give if not half of your attention, then a good third to the artist at the piano. And give him or her more than perfunctory applause.

Though *lieder* is a German word do not be surprised if you hear French songs by Fauré, Duparc, Debussy, and Ravel; Russian songs by Tchaikovsky and Rachmaninoff; Norwegian songs by Grieg.

And English songs by Vaughan Williams, Ireland, Howells, Finzi and Britten — too often neglected by European singers.

Listening to the language you understand best, you will be struck by the fact that composers dislike long, complex sentences. What appeals to them most is a phrase like:

> So we'll go no more a-roving
>   By the light of the moon.

They are attracted by:

> O, my luve's like a red, red rose
>   That's newly sprung in June!
> O, my luve's like the melodie
>   That's sweetly played in tune!

Byron and Burns.
Observe how fond German composers have been of Heine.

> Yet she who has grieved me
>   Most of all,
> She never hated
>   Nor loved me at all.

In our own century our composers made song-cycles out of A. E. Housman's poems 'A Shropshire Lad.'

> 'Give pearls away and rubies
> But keep your fancy free.'
> But I was one-and-twenty
> No use to talk to me.

The words are one or two syllables long. Simplicity and poignancy are irresistible to your song composer.

Reading such poems or listening to the songs, we cannot help reflecting that when they speak of birdsong or the sound of the stream or of a whispering wind they inhabit a world that knew nothing of farm tractors, chain saws and jet-engined aircraft. As for the simple and sentimental drawing-room ballads, so much loved by multitudes of amateur singers 50 years ago, they too belong to a relatively quiet world when it seemed possible to stride along the open road, head in the stars, dreaming of the beloved. Think of that next time you are on the motorway!

In those days the song-recital consisting of ballads and/or 'sacred' songs was a sure crowd-puller. Not now. Today the crowd follows the pop singer. It is a 'select' audience that attends a *lieder* recital. You need not hesitate to join the élite.

Be prepared on occasion to hear what is called a song-cycle. In such a work poet and composer in song after song tell of a love affair. How searching and affecting are Schubert's *Die Schöne Mullerin* (The Fair Maid of the Mill) and *Winterreise* (Winter Journey) tragic stories of hopeless love.

Schumann's *Dichterliebe* (A Poet's Love) is somewhat different. The poet Heine recovers from love, painful though it has been. He puts his grief into a large coffin and buries it.

The great composers who created the world of *lieder* are Schubert, Schumann, Brahms, Wolf and Richard Strauss. Who is the greatest? The one you are listening to.

CHAPTER NINE

OPERA AND BALLET — HISTORY AND GEOGRAPHY

Opera was Italian. Then it became French with the help of Lully (born Lulli) and Rameau. Hesitantly it became English. Purcell composed quasi-operatic pieces, also 'masques' that were a mixture of opera, ballet, and pageant. Alas that he died young: he might have founded an English operatic tradition. As it is, only the hour-long *Dido and Aenaes* is performed with any frequency. It includes that wonderful song *'When I am laid in Earth'* composed over a ground-bass — i.e. a bass melody that constantly repeats itself.

Handel arrived in London and composed Italian opera for fashionable English audiences. Italian opera was satirised in *The Beggars' Opera* . But Italian opera was regarded as *real* opera for generations afterwards.

We come to Mozart, and now there is a change. His audiences expected Italian opera but there also existed in Vienna a popular operatic entertainment in German called *Singspiel*. Dare one call it a musical? Mozart was destined to raise it to unexpected heights. Furthermore, in both Italian and German operas Mozart dared to give expression to ideas not acceptable to royal opinion. In *Le Nozze de Figaro* (Marriage of Figaro) based on a French play by Beaumarchais, sung in Italian, set in Spain, a lecherous Count is outwitted by his valet. Was that to be allowed? In *Die Zauberflöte* (The Magic Flute), sung in German and set in a fanciful Egypt, there are elements of Freemasonry. Was the Roman Catholic Church to tolerate a secret society not divulging its secrets in the confessional? In *Die Entführung aus dem Serail* (The Abduction from the Harem), sung in German and set in Turkey, a lady's maid challenges her captors saying 'I am an Englishwoman and I know my rights'. No commoner in Austria would have dared to say that. These incidents were straws in a wind that would blow up into the tempest of the French Revolution, which broke out shortly after Mozart's early death. Let us not be too political about all this, but we may observe that, as in much of his music, Mozart gives us hidden depths, not mere courtly grace and perfect form and exquisite taste. In *Don Giovanni* ('quite a Don Juan' as the lady said) we begin with an almost comic view of the wicked seducer and his hundreds of successes. But at the end we see the unrepentant Don snatched into the very flames of Hell, to the accompaniment of by no means comic music.

From this point onwards more and more operas included a nationalistic or patriotic or even revolutionary content. We cannot but be aware of this. But the extent of your awareness and how it affects your pleasure in the opera house is a matter of private judgment. Compare such operas with Shakespeare's *Julius Caesar*. One producer wants to do it in modern dress, with Marcus Antonius as mob orator leading a *coup d'état*. A different producer sees it all as wonderful oratory and splendid costume.

One thing is certain: from Beethoven's *Fidelio* (with its chorus of released political prisoners) onwards, we are made aware of 'the people' — the operatic chorus that represents the peasantry, the soldiery, the patriots, the captives, the invaders, or whatever.

How did all this begin? Let us compare *God Save the King*, a royal anthem, with *La Marseillaise*, the first truly national anthem, calling on 'Children of the Fatherland'. Nowadays both anthems may be regarded as merely ceremonial, but *La Marseillaise* sent shivers down the spine of every despotic monarch in Europe. Ironically enough it was composed by an officer and gentleman who intended it to be patriotic rather than revolutionary. What he did not realise was that, in some countries, patriotism to one's country could be regarded as disloyalty towards one's emperor. It was *his* country. The Austrian emperor wanted no Czech or Hungarian patriotism. The Tsar wanted no Polish patriotism. And what of Italian patriotism, seeing that northern Italy was ruled by Austria, middle Italy by the Pope, and southern Italy by the 'Kingdom of the Two Sicilies'?

Read any biography of Verdi and see how often he was in trouble with the Austrian police and in frequent danger of having his works banned. When Italy did at last become an independent, unified nation, Verdi for a while was a Senator. How often the villain of opera is a tyrant — Don Pizarro in Beethoven's *Fidelio*; Philip II of Spain in Verdi's *Don Carlos*, unmoved by the burning of heretics; Baron Scarpia, head of the secret police in Puccini's *Tosca*; *Boris Godounov*, usurper and half-mad tyrant in Mussorgsky's opera.

True, true! But, sitting in the opera house, we care about the human relationships of a few characters, we are affected, often unconsciously, by the orchestral sound, and we wait to be thrilled by each great aria. Was it Tito Ruffo who declared 'For opera three things are necessary. The first is voice, the second is voice, the third is voice'. You will not gain much by arguing that Madam Butterfly, seduced by an American naval officer, was a victim of imperialism, but you may lose a little by completely ignoring historical context and regarding opera as a sad love story set to music. I say 'sad' because Grand Opera is by definition tragic.

Many operas are about love and not much else. Mozart's *Cosi fan tutte* is not a love-triangle, as many operas are, but sort of half humorous, half cynical quadrilateral of two pairs of lovers. Verdi's *Otello* tells us of the dangers of jealousy. Leoncavallo's *I Pagliacci* likewise. How many operas *are* love-triangles?

If we turn to *opera buffa*, in which true love is sure to win in the end, we can very simply enjoy the frolics of Rossini's *The Barber of Seville*, in its day the most successful of all operas and still going strong.

If you go to the opera primarily for the singing — if you are a 'canary fancier' — you will certainly enjoy *coloratura* singing if it is stunningly well performed. This is the kind of singing that is full of vocal fireworks (the visual comparison is very apt). A *coloratura aria* is intended to stop the show. The audience cannot be restrained from applause. Its nearest instrumental equivalent is the cadenza in a piano or violin concerto. Sure enough, the most famous coloratura singers were and are very expensive.

In the nineteenth century the composing of opera was subject to constant evolution. Earlier there had been the clear difference between *recitativo* and *aria*. The one told the facts or carried on the plot; the other, like a Shakespeare soliloquy, explored thought and feeling, very much addressed to the audience. Here and there the composer would provide a duet or ensemble, but the divisions were pretty clear cut. In the romantic era the recitative was replaced by something much less perfunctory, a flow of composition. Nevertheless, there were still quite clearly the great arias, the hit-numbers that could be detached from the work and sung as concert items or, in the twentieth century, recorded as favourite excerpts.

During this era the musical map was broadening. Musicians became more and more conscious of nationhood. For example, it became apparent that Tchaikovsky's *Eugene Onegin* would sound not Italian but Russian even if sung in English. It was, however, a strange fact of a contrary kind that Tchaikovsky could compose an *Italian Caprice*, Brahms could compose *Hungarian Dances*, and Mendelssohn could please Queen Victoria with a *'Scotch'* Symphony and the *Hebrides* ('Fingal's Cave') overture. Were there two kinds of nationalism — the one genuine and the other a kind of musical fancy dress?

Let us digress from the subject of opera for a moment. In every country a musical child was certain to imbibe the nursery tunes and the folk songs of his own people. They constituted a kind of musical landscape, one that was different from anyone else's. They could influence a composer unconsciously and very deeply. Nevertheless that same composer, in manhood, might take a holiday in, say, Italy and understand the idiom of a gondolier's song in Venice or a fisherman's song in Naples. He finds it possible musically to impersonate those men. He is quick to observe characteristic rhythms, oft-repeated harmonies, certain turns of phrase. Travelling further he is aware that the basic chords heard on a Spanish guitar are not those of a Russian balalaika. The bagpipes of Scotland are not like those of Poland.

It is almost like learning foreign cookery — paprika in one dish, curry in another.

Consider a well-known Scottish song: *Gin a body meet a body, comin' through the rye*. The words 'body' and 'comin'' are sung in a rhythm often called the Scotch Snap. Go further. Become aware of the standardised cadences employed by a gypsy fiddler. Ask yourself if the rhythms of *flamenco* are as inimitable as they are sometimes supposed to be.

You will have to admit that borrowed nationalism can be remarkably convincing, and you will not be too surprised if, in *Carmen*, you hear wonderfully Spanish music composed by the French composer Bizet. Incidentally both Ravel and Debussy produced convincing Spanish music, and the American-Jewish Gershwin composed *Porgy and Bess*, an opera peopled by poor blacks in the Deep South.

Occasionally composers would try to transport us to far-away, exotic countries. Any child can obtain a vaguely Chinese effect by inventing tunes on nothing but the black notes of a piano.* Any orchestrator has a battery of gongs and bells to enhance the effect. But a European composer is unlikely to understand Chinese or Indian or Arabic music in any depth while marvelling at the way in which oriental people, particularly the Japanese, have adopted European music. (European instruments made in Japan are to be found all over the world.)

In the nineteenth century it was the Russian composers who most successfully brought oriental colour into European music. The empire of the Tsars, nearly as large as the empire of the Soviets, included vast populations of Mongol people in central Asia. We need not be surprised if Borodin and Rimsky-Korsakov transported us into lands that seemed scarcely real or that Diaghilev's *Ballets Russes* enabled us not only to hear Rimsky-Korsakov's *Scheherazade* but in a sense to see the stories of the Arabian Nights.

French composers were also in the field. Debussy was enchanted when he heard Balinese *gamelan* music in Paris and one of his piano pieces is called *Pagodes.* In the opera *Lakmé*, with its famous Bell Song for coloratura soprano, by Delibes and also in the opera *The Pearl Fishers* by Bizet you will find a Brahmin priest. Most of the music is obviously French, just as most of the music in Puccini's *Madam Butterfly* and *Turandot* is obviously Italian, but a suggestion of oriental colour was welcome in European and American opera houses.

In the midst of all these changes there was one composer totally uninfluenced by foreign styles, changes in fashion, or classical models. This was Wagner. He found his stories in Nordic mythology and in the adventures of medieval Christian German knights. Himself no model of Christian humility or forbearance, he was arguably the most strong-willed of all composers, fighting his way through endless intrigues and, in the end, building a theatre in which nothing was ever to be performed but his works. His is the most extraordinary life-story of all, a story that every music-lover should read.

* On the black keys there are only five notes in an octave: hence 'pentatonic' tunes.

Does an interested music-lover need to be told how to listen to Wagner or how to understand the stage-action? Perhaps yes, even though the music can make an immediately overwhelming effect. Many people who enjoy, say, the Overture to *The Mastersingers*, or *The Ride of the Valkyries*, in the concert-hall or on record, are bewildered and impatient when they first experience Wagner in the opera house. If ever there was a story-teller who takes his time . . .

A few facts and reflections, then. Wagner wrote his own *libretti* and, wishing to distance himself from other men's operas, called his works music-dramas. He prided himself on being a thinker, but was more of a visionary and sorceror. He had complex ideas about fate and destiny and the role of a good woman in the redemption of a sinful man, and there is a powerful eroticism in much of the music.

It is always advisable to read a synopsis of an operatic story before going to a performance: in the case of Wagner it is imperative. How else will you thread your way through the four music-dramas that in succession add up to *The Ring of the Nibelungs*? (They are *The Rhinegold, The Valkyrie, Siegfried,* and *The Twilight of the Gods*.) Siegfried is the young man who, owing nothing to education (in those dark forests inhabited by malevolent dwarfs, guileless giants, and cunning gods), is guided by natural courage and genius until betrayed by poisonous magic.

It is all very symbolic. Is the wicked dwarf who, preferring power to love, steals the gold from the Rhine-Maidens — is he a picture of the greedy capitalist? Is he perhaps a Jew (Wagner being a violent hater of Jews)? Are the giants the simple and basically good 'people'? Are the gods, decreeing the building of their Valhalla, the decadent ruling classes? How interesting it is that, having created Siegfried as the very epitome of the perfect, young, handsome, courageous German, Wagner's genius compelled him to bring Siegfried to a tragic end, following which (to the accompaniment of stupendous music) Valhalla goes up in flames.

Sign-posting the way through this vast epic are 'leading motives'. Each *leit-motif* is attached to a special event or person, appearing and re-appearing with powerful force at appropriate moments . . . the ring motive, the curse motive, the magic-sword motive, the Valhalla motive. Nobody can explain why each of these short, pregnant phrases seems so perfect for its purpose.

Wagner's music weaves an uninterrupted tapestry, making great use of interrupted cadences that seem to say 'not yet' again and again. No 'hit-number' arias. No-one had a greater command of melting discords suggesting either rapture or anguish, and no earlier composer had used such a rich orchestration. Singing teachers denounced this orchestral force as death to the voice. It may seem that history has proved them wrong, but the music has in fact proved dangerous to all but the strongest and most mature voices.

All this may seem to suggest that Wagner is too complex and long-winded to appeal to big audiences. Not so. Wagner lived to see people from distant countries making what was almost a pilgrimage to his theatre at Bayreuth. Almost every one of his works is a sell-out, often at enhanced prices.

There was a time, during and after the second world-war, when people who had suffered under the Nazis found Wagner hard to take. (Hitler loved Bayreuth, and Bayreuth loved Hitler.) But Wagner remains the great spell-binder.

Approaching Wagner for the first time, you might be well advised to try *Lohengrin* or *Tristan and Isolde*.

Wagner thought he was composing the 'Music of the Future'. There came a time, inevitably, when so powerful a music engendered a powerful reaction, but there is no denying Wagner's influence on Richard Strauss and Mahler.

The one composer of his era who could, so to speak, stand up to Wagner was Verdi. Though he deployed a bigness and energy not to be found in earlier composers like Rossini, Bellini and Donizetti, he was never accused of being death to the voice. He never forgot that mellifluous quality called *bel canto*. The singers loved him. He was immensely successful with such works as *Il Trovatore, La Traviata, Aida* (with its opportunities for sumptuous production) and many others. In old age he composed *Otello* and, in yet older age, followed this tragedy by the sparkling *Falstaff* (derived from *The Merry Wives of Windsor*). He died very rich.

In passing we may note how many Italian operas are based on the plays of Shakespeare or the novels of Sir Walter Scott.

Later and still richer there was Puccini. It needs a heart of stone to resist *La Bohème* and *Madam Butterfly*.

Once captured by opera, you have a vast repertoire to explore. Speaking of a particular work you will probably say *La Traviata* rather than The Frail One; *Rosenkavalier* rather than Cavalier of the Rose; *Otello* rather than Othello. But you will refer to The Bartered Bride rather than *Prodana Nevesta* while remembering to emphasise the first syllable of the composer's name, Smetana; you will probably say Magic Flute rather than *Zauberflöte,* remembering to pronounce Mozart as Moat-zart, and it might be as well, when referring to *Don Giovanni,* to remember than Gio- is pronounced not gee-oh but jo, while -vanni should rhyme with the southern-English pronunciation 'funny'. Nobody refers to *La Bohème* as The Bohemians, but almost everybody says Eugene Onegin rather than *Evgeny Onegin*, and The Tales of Hoffman rather than *Les Contes d'Hoffman*. Always remember that the middle syllable of *Tannhäuser* is "hoy, not 'how', and please speak English rather than French when referring to *Samson et Dalila* even though you remember not to sound the *d* in the name Gounod.

A few more pronunciations may be noted if, by chance, you do not know them already, *Dvořák:* Vorjahk; *Kodály:* Co-dye; *Strauss:* Shtrowse. The waltz-kings, father and son, shared *Johann* Yohahn, a name that also belongs to Johann Sebastian Bach (pronounce the *ch* as in the Scottish loch). With Richard Strauss be content to say *Richard* in the English fashion unless you can manage *R* in the throat, a *ch* that is unlike our own ch or sh, and a final *d* that is pronounced like our t. The three syllables of *Debussy* should be said with nearly equal stress and the word should not rhyme with juicy. For *Schoenberg* Shernberg will do. The ü in *Walküre* can be managed if you purse your lips into an o-shape and then try to say e. The Spanish *Falla* is something like Fie-ya. Though *Chopin* was a Polish patriot you may remember that his father was French: pronounce accordingly. *Liszt* can be called List, and *Sibelius* is Sibaylius. You will not need to be told about Baithoven, and doubtless you already say High-dn.

Let us return to opera and ballet.

If anybody in an opera house mentions the *répétiteur* you should know that he is referring to a rehearsal pianist — the very competent musician who makes sure that the singers, whether solo or in the chorus, know the score properly.

On the whole, the opera house is the home of romantic theatre. In our modern times however, we have learned to accept that Stravinsky's *Rake's Progress* and Berg's two operas *Wozzeck* and *Lulu* are anti-romantic. (Schoenberg's *Moses und Aaron* is something of a staged oratorio.) And, buying our tickets for the operas of Britten, we know we shall not be treated to love-duets.

Buying tickets for the ballet you must be prepared to use some new words. What is called Classical Ballet is danced to music of the romantic era. Some examples have survived with third-rate music (e.g. *Giselle* to the music of Adam) but there is no need to be condescending to *Swan Lake* or *Sleeping Beauty* with music by Tchaikovsky.

Russia was the great home of ballet until that extraordinary impresario and talent scout, Diaghilev, formed his *Ballets Russes*, a troupe that never performed in Russia. He chose, he inspired, he bullied new young composers, choreographers and designers and inaugurated a new era. We shall come to him in the chapter on Modern Music.

Meanwhile we may note that many ballets are peopled not by human beings but by magicians, puppets, fairies, demon kings and spellbound princes.

CHAPTER TEN

ORCHESTRAS, CONDUCTORS, INTERPRETATION

Once upon a time musical instruments were simple — the hunting horn, the shepherd's pipe, the minstrel's harp.

Let us begin with the brass. In simple form a brass instrument is very much imprisoned in one key. Even in the scores of classical composers you will find Horn in D, Horn in E flat, Horn in F.* In the course of a symphony, during a period of silence, the player of those days would detach a section of piping, fit alternative piping into place, and then continue. This was called changing the crook. The invention of valves made this unnecessary. Even so, the horn of today is usually 'in F' which means that F is, so to speak, the C-major of his instrument. In other words, the player's C-scale sounds like the F-scale to everyone else . . . a fifth lower than what's written. The composer who wants us to hear the scale of C must write it a fifth higher, in the scale of G. There are other transposing instruments. Learning to play the clarinet, you will probably begin on a B-flat instrument: later you will have to buy an A instrument as well. There are also families of trumpets.

The trombones, equipped with telescopic slides, always had more freedom of the keys.

It is a basic fact that the bigger the instrument, the lower the pitch. Most instruments have a bottom floor: you can go no lower. Upper range depends to some degree on the player's skill.

Some instruments need constant attention. Wood-wind players are bothered about reeds, string players about strings. (Flutes have no reeds.) Watch and listen and you will discover that the single-reed clarinets sound less 'reedy' than the double-reed oboe, cor anglais, or bassoon. (The cor anglais is neither a horn nor English: it is a lower voiced oboe.)

During the evolution of the wood-wind instruments various inventors improved the action. By means of what some people call 'the saltspoons' a player could put a finger *here* and open or close a hole *there*.

Early in the last century Sebastien Erard added seven pedals to the harp. He also very much improved piano action with his double escapement.

---

*This elaborately coiled instrument was developed in France. Hence 'French Horn'. An English french-horn may have a slightly different tone from a German french-horn. However, one says 'horn-player', not french-horn player.

Adolphe Sax, a Belgian in Paris, invented the saxhorn and the saxophone. This last has a conical tube like an oboe, a single reed as in a clarinet, and a tube of brass. Little did Sax realise that in the days of the misnamed jazz bands it would wail its melodies across every ballroom. (It doesn't have to wail: it only learned how to.)

The composers welcomed every improvement — particularly Berlioz. He wrote a treatise on what he called *Instrumentation* — we now say orchestration — and declared that the orchestra could express the soul of a nation. French governments gave him commissions to compose enormous pieces for state occasions. As concert halls and opera houses grew larger, so did orchestras. On stage, outsize voices were required, and audiences learned to accept a two-ton soprano impersonating a youthful and beautiful heroine.

As orchestras grew larger, the percussion instruments grew more numerous.

In many Victorian halls, at the back of the stage, towering over the orchestra was the organ, the *grand* organ with three, four, or even five keyboards (manuals) for the hands, another for the feet, and innumerable stops to produce variety of tone, the basic tone being 'diapason'. Gazing at the serried ranks of pipes, few music lovers could have guessed that, one day, there would be organs without any pipes at all, or that there would be a brief era of theatre organs and cinema organs.

Contemplating all these musical machines you must surely be struck by the relativity of such words as loud and soft. A tiny piccolo can be heard above all other sounds. A side drum makes a more shattering noise than any of the timpani. Violas 'blend in' while trumpets stand out. It is nice to have plenty of strings, but eight cellos never seem to be eight times as loud as one.

There is no need for the listener to be able to spot every instrument during a performance, but you will, as a concert-goer, begin to distinguish the brass from the wood-wind, and you will never mistake the strings for the percussion. If you rely mostly on your record-player or cassette-deck, buy Britten's *Young Person's Guide to the Orchestra*, a beautiful and instructive set of variations on a theme by Purcell. Also listen to the 3rd movement of Tchaikovsky's 4th symphony which begins with *pizzicato* (plucked) strings, goes on to wood-wind with horns, and then gives you all the brass plus timpani (tuned kettle-drums).

Orchestras come in various sizes, from the chamber orchestra of, say, 20 players to the full symphony orchestra or opera-house orchestra of more than a hundred, not to mention the special orchestras that play for musicals, make sound-tracks for films, assemble in television studios.

In this connection one must make several points about orchestration. The composer of a symphony orchestrates 'ideally', hoping that his work will be played by famous orchestras. But there are musicians, not necessarily composers, who are specialist orchestrators. In the days of 'the big band', every band-leader had his resident orchestrator who knew how to create the recognisable sound for which the band was famous. He not only orchestrated for the band: he had in mind particular players — Tommy on trumpet or Benny on sax.

It is said that great composers know how to think orchestrally. Maybe, but Ravel published several works for piano first and for orchestra afterwards. Did he arrange for piano in order to ensure publication, or did he write for piano and then decide to orchestrate?

Orchestration can have a cosmetic effect, making an unremarkable idea sound better than it deserves.

Let us now consider conductors, but first make a note of this: the front man of the first violins is, in Britain, the leader of the orchestra. In America he is the concert-master. The British conductor on the rostrum is transformed in America into the leader on the podium. Two different meanings for 'leader' can be puzzling.

Conducting, as we know it now, is not a very old-established activity. When Haydn came to London he would sit at a piano, though no piano part was written in the score, and intervene from time to time to hold the players together. Meanwhile, the first violinist sometimes played and sometimes waved his bow in the air. All the players but the cellists stood up, throughout the concert.

Who first conducted in the modern style? No historian can say for certain, but one pioneer was the violinist-composer Ludwig Spohr who alarmed the Philharmonic Society in London by taking a baton from his pocket and proposing to direct the performance with its aid. It seems that conducting was not at first as busy as it later became. It is said that Mendelssohn conducted only at certain moments, intervening when necessary.

Looking at the whole business of conducting, we may well wonder whether there is such a thing as conducting technique. Whereas violinists move their bows up and down in unison and in much the same style, each conductor seems to have invented his own individual repertoire of gestures. This impression is deceptive. Something of the art of conducting can be taught. For one thing, a student-conductor must learn score-reading.

See how much is written to produce just the chords marked:

Our student-conductor must discover how to convey rhythm with one hand while suggesting expressiveness with the other. He must conduct groups of fellow students and learn how to glance at players who have been temporarily silent so as to 'bring them in'. This alertness can, of course, be overdone, but a student's conductor-teacher is liable to tell the old story of the provincial choirmaster who longed to conduct a symphony orchestra. At last the opportunity came and the rehearsal began. A crash of cymbals. Angrily he looked up and said 'Oo done that?'

Inevitably conductors began to be spectacular. There was the Frenchman, Louis Antoine Jullien, a pioneer of Promenade Concerts in London, who bedazzled his worshipping audiences with a jewelled baton. He always put on fresh white gloves for a Beethoven symphony. After enormous success he became poor and died mad. This is not the customary fate of successful conductors. Some have married yet again at the age of 80 and have finally collapsed, still waving their arms, at 90.

Some conductors give the impression of dancing to the music, but the object of the enterprise is that the music should dance to the conductor. If ever, at home, secretly, you have waved your arms at a record-player do please realise that the machine is conducting you.

A good teacher can train an intelligent student to be competent, but the best conductors are 'naturals'. There are many stories of musicians who, in an emergency, leapt on to the rostrum, took over, and began a career.

In a small way this happened to me. During the Hitler war, at a time when I had engagements to play piano concertos with the London Philharmonic Orchestra, I was asked by the orchestral manager if I would conduct children's concerts. I had never conducted a symphony orchestra in my life — indeed I had scarcely ever conducted at all — but he assured me that I would be all right. 'Most conductors don't know how to talk to an audience of children. You do; and you're a good musician, and it's all well known music — things like the Flying Dutchman overture, perhaps one movement of a Tchaikovsky symphony . . . maybe the leader can play the Mendelssohn fiddle concerto . . . that sort of thing . . .'

I became the instant conductor. How good? 'Well,' said a player who had known some very great conductors, 'you're not bad'. I did not kid myself that I was, or would become, a great conductor: I knew that a real conductor must start very young and I was already in mid-career as a pianist, but I had something of that mysterious possession called a gift and of that equally mysterious quality called authority.

From that experience I feel able to say that the truly great conductors fascinate us because we can see so much yet see so little. It's all on display, but we don't know how it's done.

For example: Beethoven's Fifth Symphony is very difficult to start. Think of saying 'Run along to there.' Now omit the first word and say 'along to there'. The conductor has to beat on the inaudible 'run' and again on 'there'. To get that done with unanimity, from cold, is never easy. It doesn't look hard but it is so. However, the legendary Fürtwangler seemed to go into a preliminary convulsion that shook him from top to toe. When this ceased, the Berlin Philharmonic played the beginning perfectly. I could never see how.

Sometimes a chance remark gives us a clue to a conductor's thinking. Sir Henry Wood, the founder of London's still continuing Promenade Concerts: 'The sign of a first rate conductor is that he can make a third rate orchestra sound like a second rate orchestra.' Sir Thomas Beecham, in his seigneurial fashion: 'I hire the best men and let them play.' Leonard Bernstein tells of his encounters with two great conductors when he was a young man taking conducting courses. Maestro No. 1 calls out 'Mr Bernstein, what is the second bassoon doing in bar 201?' Mr Bernstein looks at the score to find out. 'Mr Bernstein, if you do not know what the bassoon is doing, by what right are you conducting this piece?' Now Maestro No. 2: 'You know, my boy, it is very difficult to conduct this work if you have never walked along the banks of the Volga by moonlight.'

I quote from a possibly faulty memory of one of Bernstein's television programmes, but the essence is there: 1) technique, 2) imagination.

If a conductor gives an unusual 'reading' of a work do the players ever say '*That* can't be right surely?' Once again we must think of the mysterious quality of authority. The verdict may be 'When *he* does it, it seems O.K.'.

No conductor is great in everything: '. . . marvellously controlled, you hear every note, but no heroine is going to die of love to the sound of *that*.' Alternatively: 'I do wish he'd sometimes *not* try to sweep you off your feet.'

Then again 'These great conductors are all very well, but when it comes to baroque music you really must listen to the *Gott-in-Himmel* ensemble from Handelbach-am-Rhein. Such a joy when violins stop that endless vibrato, don't you think?'

There are conductors who succeed in the concert hall but not in the opera house. Others who command in both. There was a time when an opera conductor was god. Nowadays the producer is a rival deity. You may sometimes find that the stage picture does not agree with the sound picture.

The opera conductor drives the performance along overall, yet he must defer to the singers when soprano and tenor are singing their love duet — deferring but not depriving them of support. Singers may prolong a top note but they do not stop on it. The baton hovers like a seagull in the wind, deceptively still.

A few generations ago conductors were somehow more wilful than they are today. ('*My* interpretation is quite different.') Every time the music turned a corner, the tempo changed even though no change was indicated in the score. Later there was the doctrine of the great arch of development — the farsighted view that forbade any hanging about. There will always be dogma, doctrine and fashion and it is advisable not to be over-influenced by what is called informed critical opinion.

As for authenticity and faithfulness to the text I should mention that when Rachmaninoff composed his second piano concerto he marked a certain cadenza to be played soft, fairly loud, loud, very loud. In his own recording he reversed everything and played very loud, less loud, soft, very soft. What would *you* do if you were a pianist?

Some conductors insist on observing every indicated repeat. For my part, I sometimes find it tiresome when, just as I am expecting to begin the development, I am compelled to listen to the exposition all over again. How dare I disobey Beethoven? Well, when Ferdinand Ries decided to play the Hammerklavier Sonata in London, Beethoven suggested certain omissions to help the English audience. 'You could omit the Largo and begin straightaway with the Fugue . . . or you could use the first movement and then the Adagio . . . and omit entirely number four . . . or you could take just the first movement and the Scherzo and let them form the whole sonata. I leave it to you to do what you think best.'

Maybe Beethoven was over-anxious to be heard in London, and we would not now cut chunks out of one of his works. But we may usefully recall that, at the piano, he never played a piece twice the same way. Today we are strait-jacketed by the record. If you buy a certain conductor's recording of a symphony and then go to see him in the flesh, will you not expect a performance like the one you already know?

Always there is the problem of expression marks. In his piano sonata in G minor Schumann indicates 'as fast as possible'. At the end of the movement, at the top of the last page, we read 'yet faster'. As a student I was advised to translate *andante* as meaning leisurely. What can *andantino* mean? A little bit leisurely? In Italian the word *allegro* means merry. Not so in music. What about *allegro con fuoco*? To play the *allegro* with fire you need something other than merriment. At the end of this book you will find a glossary with some comments on vague meanings. Never say 'What a pity they couldn't be more precise'.

It is said that when Mahler — great conductor and great composer — wanted to indicate a very slightly slower tempo he would indicate *nicht eilen* — don't hurry. And it has always been open to a composer to write *tempo giusto* which I am tempted to translate as a just-so tempo.

It might be argued that in our modern age we have records of performances conducted by the composers themselves. Britten was an admirable conductor. Look in television archives for his *Billy Budd* played under his direction — have we not the definitive performance of the opera? The next generation will certainly not think so. What about stereoscopic vision, digital sound, and, instead of a sailing ship (a man o'war) a space-craft in orbit? You can be sure that the tempi and the accents will alter.

In a recording studio a conductor is never quite his public self. He listens to a take. He decides to re-take a few passages. From the highest music to the lowest there is the process of packaging the product. There is an inhuman demand for accuracy. What customer will buy a record if there is a wrong note that will be increasingly irritating if the record is in frequent use? (We shall think more about packaging when we come to light music.)

If, interested in interpretation, you read critiques, always remember that the 'crit' you read may be roundly contradicted in another newspaper or magazine.

CHAPTER ELEVEN

THE VIRTUOSI

The pianoforte is far and away the most influential of instruments. More great music has been written for it than for all the others put together. No doubt the orchestra has an enormous repertoire, but an orchestral instrumentalist playing solo has a very small repertoire compared with that of a pianist. Just one example: Beethoven composed thirty-two sonatas and five concertos for piano. Match that, you fiddlers and cellists and wind players!

Furthermore a singer or instrumentalist needs a piano for accompaniments. And composers have always needed a piano as a test-bed on which to try out their ideas, even if composing was done away from the piano. (Beethoven liked going out for a walk, sketch-book in hand.)

Many composers have been pianist-composers: Mozart, Beethoven, Liszt, Chopin, Mendelssohn, Rachmaninoff. Piano makers have vied with one another to please these great men. In America the firm of Steinway and Sons, over a number of years, promoted piano recitals on their own instruments, of course.

I must not seem to say that only pianists are virtuosi. After all, it was the legendary violinist Paganini who inspired the young Liszt to aspire to similar heights of performance — both men being masters of showmanship. And, of course, there have been, and are, great cellists, viola players, organists, guitar players, flute players, not to mention players of the harmonica and accordion.

For some unexplained reason, infant prodigies are nearly always pianists or violinists. The mind boggles at the idea of an infant bass player.

Virtuoso playing is much more common than it used to be, partly because elderly virtuosi have taught young ones (Liszt generously gave free classes to groups of young hopefuls), and nowadays because records give the growing youngster ever-present examples of what can be done.

Virtuosity should be neither over nor under-rated. It can be a temptation to the highly skilled pianist or violinist who puts a display piece at the end of the programme to make sure of cries of *Encore*. It took a Schnabel to say 'The difference between me and other pianists is that *my* programmes are boring all the way through'. There is no reason why you should not clap like mad if a violinist strikes sparks from his Strad when he plays Paganini caprices or when a pianist plays those Etudes that Liszt dared to call *Studies in Transcendental Execution*.

It may be argued that there is more pianism than music in such works, but the great merit of virtuosity is that it makes a man free to play such an enormous and profound work as Beethoven's Hammerklavier sonata. Pianists are fortunate in having many pieces that are as wonderfully musical as they are excitingly pianistic; a comment that applies to most of Chopin's music. Your pianist can play Schumann's *Etudes Symphoniques* (why symphonic, I wonder?), Brahms's *Variations on a theme by Paganini*, Liszt's one and wonderful sonata, not to mention Rachmaninoff's *Preludes* and transcriptions.

Some severe critics look askance at transcriptions. It must be admitted that some of Liszt's — not all — are 'a bit naughty'. In fairness, however, it must also be said that, through his piano versions of symphonies, *lieder*, organ works, and so on, Liszt promoted a great many pieces that were still unknown or controversial. Living in the age when everything was 'tried over' on the piano, he was enormously persuasive.

As for later transcriptions, I recall asking a Cambridge don what he thought of Bach-Busoni. He recoiled in the way I expected, but then recovered enough to ask my own opinion. I said 'When the summer comes, you floodlight your beautiful colleges. The effect is theatrical: they become almost like stage-sets. One sees them as one never saw them before. In the autumn you switch off. No harm has been done'. He managed to say 'I take your point'.

How much should you care about authenticity? There are those who would like Mozart's music to be played on a small, period, 'square' piano. But Mozart himself arranged Bach keyboard fugues for string quartet, and he re-orchestrated Handel's *Messiah*. Certainly it is interesting to hear a Beethoven sonata played on a 'fortepiano' i.e. a wooden-frame piano with its hammers tipped with leather, not felt. Its strings ran straight from front to back, not as in the modern grand where the bass strings run, so to speak, S.W. to N.E. while the treble strings, S.E. to N.W., cross over them (overstrung) thereby increasing the length of the strings.

It is, I think, important to hear baroque music on a harpsichord and, if you like, organ music on a baroque-style organ.

To return to virtuosity — I am reminded of the quip that an artist is a neurotic who knows how to use his neurosis. It can fairly be said that a virtuoso is obsessional and perfectionist. Practising he may seem introverted: performing he seems extroverted. Some people think that he practises eight hours a day (never seven or nine). There are pianists who are incessant practisers, even practising on an upright piano in the artist's room during the interval of a recital. Others are like the pianist who said 'Eight hours a day? Whatever for? I *know* how to play the piano'.

The old-time pianists and fiddlers and singers went out of their way to look the part. Some bowed with an imperious nod: others very deeply, hand on heart. Some fussed endlessly over the height of the piano stool. There were aloof violinists; there were those who, almost like gypsies, played to the women. There were sopranos famed for *couture* and *coiffure* — and for a certain amplitude of *taille.*

If there is less showmanship now, it is because, for much of the time, artists are invisible, broadcasting or recording. With the microphone taking it all down in evidence for the benefit of the critics, there is great emphasis on literal accuracy, perfect tuning, exact faithfulness to the text. Much has been gained but something has been lost.

What of the virtuosity and showmanship of light musicians? We shall come to that later. But at this point we need to consider the piano as a special case. How do you play *crescendo* (increasing the tone gradually) on an instrument where every note produces a *diminuendo* (a decreasing sound)? How does your right hand bring out the melody, if the bass strings are long and heavy, producing sounds that take quite a while to die away? Seeing that a hammer is flung toward the strings and bounces off, is there any point in deploying a caressing touch?

Listening to a pianist, always remember that on a pianoforte one plays *piano* and *forte* at the same time. 'Bring out the melody' is an instruction that may best be obeyed by making the accompaniment quiet *even in a forte phrase.* Another point: a long note in the treble must be played loudly enough, even in a soft piece, for you to be able to hear not just the beginning of the note but the end of it. It follows that short notes may be played with a certain lightness even in a fortissimo passage. What a lot of disobedience there is in interpretation! Or should one say that interpretation is a higher or deeper obedience? Of all virtuosi, the pianist is most thoroughly a conjuror, deploying the sleight of hand that deceives the ear. Ask yourself what is the difference between intimate softness and the other sort of softness that suggests loudness in the distance?

In this matter of conjuring — deceiving the ear of the listener — we must also think of voice production. After the opera you may hear enthusiastic voices declaring that the *diva* floated a wonderful pianissimo over the audience that could be thrillingly enjoyed in the back row of the furthest balcony. Not so. A literal softness cannot cross a hundred-piece orchestra and reach all the people from row-A to row-Z. No: the singer's pianissimo is like the actor's stage-whisper. Talk to singers and their teachers and you will hear many theories about resonance and projection and you will also realise what a mysterious thing A Voice is compared with your voice or mine. A Voice is not an instrument. Instruments can be bought, and discarded if unsatisfactory.

Listening to a singer you respond to the personal, recognisable quality of the voice, its ability to project character, not just ever-so-beautiful tone, the impression at a climax of having power in reserve, its ease with high and low notes, its perfect tuning.

Alas, there are canaries who can be beguiling but never dramatic; there are character-singers who must be confined to playing old men, demented witches, and suchlike; there are heavenly oratorio singers who had better not attempt opera, and opera singers whose *lieder* singing is ridiculous. And there are singers who, knowing that vocal tone emerges on vowels, are quite contemptuous of consonants, leaving you wondering whether the language is Sanskrit. They do not realise that, confronted by 'I love you', they must sing 'I lah . . . view'. You must learn the conventions. For example, no gesture in *lieder* singing: only facial expression.

Returning to the instrumentalists — do not applaud between movements of a sonata or concerto. Understand that, despite the difficulties of memorisation, a pianist may feel that he plays better without the page, especially as eyes-on-keyboard may be advantageous. After all, a keyboard is almost as long as a man's outstretched arms. And is there not better communication between a violinist and audience if he is not half hidden by a music-stand?

There is a convention that oratorio singers may hold a score in their hands (giving their hands something to do?). Conventions in dress may alter, but they are important. While you admire the artist, you expect the artist to show his respect for you by looking the part.

Virtuosity attracts audiences. At the end of a great performance by a star violinist people emerge from the concert hall talking excitedly. 'Wasn't he wonderful! Did you ever hear such beautiful tone? And that cadenza . . . God, what a technique . . .'

You, no doubt, are attracted by famous players and, maybe, have said to a friend 'You mean you were not *there*?!' But ask yourself a question. If in your city a great violinist is to play the Beethoven concerto (which you love) on a Monday, and a good but less famous man is to play the Berg (which you do not know) on the Tuesday, and you cannot afford to go to both concerts, which performance will you attend?

CHAPTER TWELVE

MODERN MUSIC

When Schumann composed his *Carnaval* he called the last section 'March of the Davidites against the Philistines'. The Davidites were his friends, the moderns; the Philistines preferred, perhaps, Haydn. 'Twas ever thus and always will be.

The general pattern has been that a 'revolutionary' composer — provided he does not die young — has a few years of struggle followed by years of admiration and success. (This is true of the geniuses: not of those who are for ever composing manifestos rather than music.) As in earlier times, our own century has seen a great resistance to the most advanced ideas. You may well wonder why.

Something very radical in the way of change began to happen in the early years. The music of Debussy, Stravinsky, and Bartok gave notice of a breakdown in tonality. This was not immediately obvious. A piece might still be written in the key of three flats or four sharps or whatever, but there could be passages of bi-tonality. Imagine a pianist playing on the white keys with one hand and on the blacks with the other. This is, no doubt, an over-simple example, but there began to be a clash of keys that made some listeners say 'It sets my teeth on edge'. And when they saw the title of one of Bartok's early piano pieces — *Allegro Barbaro* — they said 'Well, of course . . .' And when Stravinsky's *Rite of Spring* appeared — the ballet depicting primitive man dancing during blood sacrifice — there was a riot in the theatre.

What of Debussy? He is labelled Impressionist, not Romantic. He seems to say 'look at the beautiful sunset' but he does not add 'oh, how it makes me think of my beloved'. With him, aesthetic sensibility often seems more important than heartfelt emotion. I suggest this cautiously since it is in the very nature of music to invite us to fall in love with what we hear.

It is true that his one opera *Pelléas et Mélisande* is a love story, but at the very moment when the lovers admit their love there is no passionate duet. The music actually stops, and they speak, murmuringly, 'I love you' . . . 'I also'. Then the music resumes. Much of Debussy's music seems devoid of human beings. His seascapes have no sailors, his Cakewalk is danced by a Golliwog, a piece may be called Footsteps in the Snow, but whose? He tells us that the Submerged Cathedral 'emerges little by little from the mist' and we can only assume that the bells are rung and the chorale is sung by ghosts — fortissimo. The mist returns, the sounds die away . . . The title of that piece is printed, not at the top of the first page but at the bottom of the last, like this, in parenthesis, after three dots (. . . *La Cathédrale Engloutie*). This eccentric behaviour is to be found in all the *Preludes* (original edition). Debussy's most popular orchestral piece is *Afternoon of a Faun* — no human beings in sight.

How beautiful the sounds are! (How beautiful the light is in an Impressionist painting.) *L'Aprés-midi d'un Faune* has wonderful continuity, but many of Debussy's pieces have a very elusive line.

Inevitably Debussy is paired with Ravel. They have many characteristics in common. You should listen for their differences. Ravel composed *Daphnis and Chloe, The Child and the Spells, Mother Goose.* His is often a more direct appeal than Debussy's. He composed concertos. His *Bolero* is a real barnstormer — the longest crescendo on record. I think you will hear a certain affinity between the two French composers and the Russian Rimsky-Korsakov whose *Scheherazade* became one of the triumphs of Diaghilev's *Ballets Russes.*

There were composers who resisted the new modernisms. Rachmaninoff continued to be 'late romantic'. When *he* announced a first performance, the public did not stay away.

The public did recoil from Arnold Schoenberg. Not at first. He began as a follower of Wagner but then realised that that territory had been over-cultivated. To the dismay of many he wrote music in no key — atonal music. Avoiding key-signatures* he inevitably avoided obvious concords. Nothing but discords! He and his admirers were, for a period of years, almost a secret society.

Going further he asked the world to accept 'Serial' music based on a note-row. As teacher and theoretician he sought structure and order, to the bewilderment of most music-lovers, some of whom thought that *tonreihe* meant tone-row. What, then, *is a* note-row?

Between a note and its octave there are twelve notes. In his first totally serial piece Schoenberg put them in this order: C-sharp, A, B, G, A-flat, F-sharp, A-sharp, D, E, E-flat, C, F. These notes were not announced as a theme or motto or subject. They were indeed concealed from the listener; but their order was maintained through the piece. No: they were not played and then played again. Any note could be transposed to a higher or lower octave. Note-lengths could be tremendously varied. While notes one-two-three were being played in the treble, one after the other, notes ten-eleven-twelve might be sounded simultaneously in the bass. Certain devices were borrowed from baroque practice. The order could be reversed or, in the Bachian sense, inverted.

Schoenberg had two pupils of genius — Berg and Webern. The three of them constitute the New Viennese School. They were not helped by either the Nazis or the Communists. The Nazis said the new music was bolshevist: the communists said it was bourgeois. In due course, Schoenberg, like his contemporary Bartok, took refuge in America.

* See Glossary

Though the first fully serial piece was called *Waltz*, the prevailing impression of serial music generally was one of nervous sensibility and anguish.

It has taken a long time for such music to find its audience, but atonal operas are now important events: Schoenberg's *Moses and Aaron,* and Berg's *Wozzeck* and *Lulu.*

By way of approach you may like to begin with early works. Schoenberg's *Transfigured Night* or *Pierrot Lunaire.* You may feel that Berg's Violin Concerto is not too far removed from the romantic concertos of earlier times.

How you react to any form of *avant-garde* music may depend to some degree on your age: the young are not too set in their ways. Nevertheless I recall an incident from years ago. I was practising some serial music. In the room with me was my son, then an infant, playing with his toys on the floor. Suddenly he stopped, came over to me, plucked my sleeve, and said 'Daddy, play properly'.

One more example of music to puzzle traditionalists. Stockhausen has a piece that must be read from a large sheet of cardboard. On this are printed a number of short fragments of music. A tempo indication is printed at the *end* of each. The pianist chooses a fragment at random. At the end of it he reads the tempo-mark and then plays his next random choice accordingly. And so on until all are played. It follows from this procedure that if, a day later, the pianist goes through the pieces in random order, yesterday's fast piece may be played slowly today.

We now live in an era when some composers are deeply involved with sounds generated electronically — no ordinary instruments. Synthesisers and computers abound.

Listen seriously — more than once. Beware of charlatans, think twice before climbing on to a band wagon, but don't, if you are young, refuse to take notice. Many pieces will die the death, but you will live to proclaim the survivors.

One curious aspect of modern music is a lessening of national character. It seems impossible to compose nostalgic or patriotic music by computer. A degree of mysticism may be apparent in some kinds of our contemporary music but not plain, traditional worship. Another problem is the ever extending musical map. We may be aware of American, German, French, Italian music. What of music from South America, India, the Far East, Africa? Is Israeli music near-eastern or is it European? How shall one know?

The communist countries have proved to be musically conservative. As a listener you will not find difficulty in enjoying the music of Prokofiev or Shostakovitch. As for Kabalevksy and Khachaturian, they catch the ear very easily. Certainly changes are taking place throughout the *bloc*, but the official, musical establishment is not eagerly receptive. Several distinguished musicians have opted out and live in the west. There seems to be only a little traffic in the other direction.

Every composer with new ideas hopes to find powerful friends and patrons. In the earlier days of our century, nobody was more influential than Serge Diaghilev, a patron who needed patronage. Not himself a dancer or composer or painter, he magnetically collected around him wonderful dancers, choreographers, artists in decor, and the greatest composers of the time. The result was his *Ballets Russes* that never danced in Russia. His radical and challenging spectacles may have been in some sense revolutionary, but they attracted royalty, the aristocracy, the world of wealth and fashion. Diaghilev was always on the edge of bankruptcy — he was always extravagant — but there was always a millionairess to come to his rescue. They listened — as they might not otherwise have listened — to music by Stravinsky, Falla, Debussy, Ravel, Richard Strauss . . .

Not everybody approved. There were those who discerned subversion, pornography, the downfall of all that was sacred, but the influence of Diaghilev in the development of modern music is incalculable.

Once, wondering what to do next, he discussed possibilities with that versatile artist Cocteau. They decided they must have another meeting. Diaghilev's parting words were 'Jean, surprise me!' This moment is worth remembering. You must distinguish between the illuminating surprise and the other kind that is merely sensational.

CHAPTER THIRTEEN

LIGHT MUSIC

It is the object of light music to appeal as quickly as possible to as many as possible. As for its value, one can always say 'Give it time and see what survives'. Nevertheless it would be foolish for the serious music-lover to dismiss it all as not worth consideration.

There is no fixed frontier between light music and 'serious' (heavy?) music. Light music can be tearful: serious music can be light-hearted. Why should we describe *The Blue Danube* as light music and the *Nutcracker* ballet music as serious? Listen, however, to both and you begin to realise that Johann Strauss could never have composed anything like the *Symphonie Pathétique,* while Tchaikovsky was a long way removed from *Die Fledermaus* (The Bat).

As for performers, how shall we put them into categories, seeing that a number of orchestral players find it quite easy to take part in an opera in the evening and to record a television jingle the next morning? Here we meet a problem concerned with respect. There are certain masterpieces of light music that deserve and sometimes attract musical devotion. Great opera companies perform *The Merry Widow* by Léhar, *Orpheus in the Underworld* by Offenbach, *Porgy and Bess* by Gershwin. Perhaps they ought to perform the Gilbert and Sullivan operettas. We accept that when an important musical is mounted there may be very competent musicians in the orchestral pit, under a skilled conductor, and we may — not too confidently — hope to hear fine voices. A fine voice is not necessarily an operatic voice. It is a matter of history that Gilbert absolutely refused to engage operatic singers. For him they were not appropriate. Let us not forget that in light opera there is spoken dialogue. The actor who really can sing is not easy to find.

We may agree that there are stage shows that deserve fine musicianship and others that get better musicianship than they deserve. In contrast we must observe that there are light musicians who are disrespectful to the composer of the music. One recalls some who transformed the melodies of Tchaikovsky and Chopin into fox-trots. One squirms to hear pop singers mauling the much loved melodies of such distinguished light composers as George Gershwin, Cole Porter, Jerome Kern, and others to the point of being almost unrecognisable. We know — do we not? — that these performances are not to be equated with variations on a theme. Having said that much, one must make something of a retreat and point out that a player of real jazz never plays a 'standard' as written. Jazz is a kind of commentary on the standard melody. There are times when it seems to belong to showbiz, yet it can also, in the right surroundings, seem like chamber music.

In the history of light music thousands and thousands of catchy tunes have been marketed — here today, gone tomorrow. One can deride them as ephemeral rubbish, but we also have to admit that only a small proportion of serious music has survival value. Look at any musical dictionary and you will see short biographies of hundreds of now forgotten composers who, in their day, were admired for their operas and symphonies and masses and chamber music. Light music sometimes lingers on in the hearts of individuals because of emotional associations. Noel Coward in *Private Lives* shows us a young divorced couple who, by chance, meet on a balcony overlooking the Mediterranean. From below there comes to their ears the sound of a band playing 'their tune' — the one they loved when they fell in love. The man says 'Extraordinary how potent cheap music is' and the phrase is especially effective in the theatre since the tune is one of Coward's own.

Mention of Noel Coward reminds us that a musically illiterate composer can 'write' songs. Coward invented his marvellously witty words and music at the piano and hired one musician to write them and another to orchestrate them. Another extraordinary example is Irving Berlin. The story goes that, like many players-by-ear, he worked in a favourite key. When the song was finished he tried it in other keys by means of a transposing piano. This now rare instrument had a keyboard that could be slid to the right or left. The keyboard moved together with the attendant hammers so that, for example, you could play on the C-major keys while the hammers hit the D-major strings, and so on.

The truth is that a successful showbiz song is essentially one idea, maybe only thirty two bars long. Conventional rhythm, fashionable harmonies, no counterpoint, no development. The composer may initially have been inspired by nothing more than a catch-phrase. The lyric writer may have fitted the words to the music. Who needs musical education?

This flippant question demands a serious answer. Let us think for a moment of Gilbert and Sullivan. Both men were educated, the one as dramatist, the other as musician*. Furthermore they wrote for reasonably well educated audiences. Listen to some of the satirical patter-songs with their many references to parliament, the judiciary, the armed forces, and you will realise that Gilbert expected his audience to know what he was talking about. G and S were not like the writers of music-hall songs about mothers-in-law.

We turn our attention to America. Besides all the European influences there are the black man's 'spirituals', the sentimental 'plantation songs' by the educated Stephen Foster, showboat music, jazz from the Deep South. The Broadway musical was born, destined to have the most powerful effect, world-wide. With the arrival of talking pictures, Broadway musicals became Hollywood musicals. These musicals, in many cases written

* How strange to mention the librettist before the composer!

70

by people whose names proclaim foreign parentage, often Jewish parentage, struck the whole world as expressing the very spirit of America, as serious American music often failed to do. Though Hollywood was intent on big profits, the studios were persuaded to allow some of the writers to be clever — not necessarily aiming at the uneducated multitude. Listen not only to the music of George Gershwin but to the words of Ira Gershwin. Listen to the music of Rodgers and admire the 'book' and the lyrics by Hammerstein. Remind yourself that *West Side Story* is a variant on the Romeo and Juliet story and was composed by that undeniably great musician, Leonard Bernstein. The American musical is one of those historic, national phenomena like German *lieder*, Italian opera, Russian ballet. We have every reason to love and admire the best of the words and music.

And we must stop and think about such words as talent and genius. It is, I think, a mistake to equate genius and greatness. Besides the great geniuses, your Beethovens and Verdis (add your own choices to the list), there are surely lesser geniuses — people whose qualities are inimitable, inexplicable, unique. And maybe there are, in all the arts, people who are occasionally visited by genius — they have their moments. Talented people are teachable: your geniuses take teachers by surprise.

You must be aware that you have several selves. You live on various levels. You talk to yourself ('I said to myself . . . '). You have a former self. A man who has no feeling for light music is denying himself.

Light music, however, presents us with a problem not much found in serious music. It could perhaps be described as the search for the even worse. If there is the faintest suggestion of intelligence or, even less acceptable, education — out! But there is a paradox here. The 'backing' by professional musicians, the packaging, the presentation require professional skill plus a certain cynicism. We can compare the marketing of some kinds of music with the exploitation of the sort of junk food that is guaranteed to rot your teeth and ruin your digestion.

Confronted with, say, the dismal spectacle of the Eurovision Song Contest, you need discrimination and a determination to recognise witty songs and brilliant performers and no others.

One more consideration demands thought. Would it be true to say that serious music is, in some fashion, middle class? The immediate, quick answer might be no. Serious music like serious literature is available to all, the one on radio and the other in the public library. And certainly there are many examples of children who, despite the poverty and ignorance of their parents, have grown up to make a valuable contribution to music. But the truth is that only a few musicians and music lovers are from the really very poor. They may recall a childhood of frugality, their parents may have been at one of the lower levels of middle class society, but there was aspiration, the desire to better oneself.

We may also recall that none of the great composers had a slum background. It is true that Nielson's father was a poor villager but he played the violin at local weddings. Verdi's father was a village shopkeeper, certainly not on the breadline. Most of the composers' fathers were musicians, schoolmasters, people connected with the stage, various kinds of professionals. And we have odd examples: Rimsky Korsakov began life as a naval officer, Mussorgsky as an army officer. Schumann's family wanted him to be a lawyer, Berlioz's a doctor.

In our modern age, when folk and traditional songs were seldom heard, when children knew advertising jingles better than nursery rhymes, when music-halls were closing their doors, was there to be no working-class voice? The Beatles arrived. They sang of Liverpool, of their local streets and clubs and the people therein. Their untrained, unrefined voices were given projection by means of microphones. They were far from brainless, and a brief genius touched them very occasionally.

What happened? The four young men who began in a cavern in a slum street became multi-millionaires, landed proprietors and owners of Rolls-Royces. And the sons and daughters of multi-millionaires, landed proprietors and owners of Rolls-Royces joined the millions of almost hysterical admirers. University men wrote theses on the new phenomenon, and someone proclaimed that Lennon and McCartney were the greatest song-writers since Schubert. You may think this an over-estimate, but what is *your* estimate? And have you any scale of values whereby you can evaluate rock, hard rock, punk rock and whatever other varieties of rock there may be? Or do you think any such evaluation a waste of time?

In the midst of all this, jazz pursues its independent way. The original jazz that was played by poor and illiterate black musicians in New Orleans developed in a way that greatly influenced show-biz, ballroom music, big band music. Such composers as Debussy, Ravel and Stravinsky were not immune from the influence of ragtime, and Gershwin attempted 'symphonic jazz' with the piano concerto he called *Rhapsody in Blue*. This is full of memorable ideas very roughly slung together. Nevertheless there persisted, through all this, what one might call *jazz* as such. And there developed a kind of playing and singing that seemed to owe almost nothing to music teachers. Great pianists went to night clubs in Chicago, sat entranced by the best jazzmen, and wondered how it was done.

In due course quite a number of serious pianists got the trick of it, but we never hear of a total jazzman who plays Beethoven sonatas.

A word about blues music: one of its characteristics is the use of minor melody notes over major harmonies, but technical analysis on paper tells us very little. The performer must have the feel for it, and the feel is easier to recognise than to describe.

Though jazz seems to exist in a world of its own, we cannot help reflecting that a gospel singer has something in common with an opera singer, that a jazz orchestra that features certain players (first one lot and then others) is playing a kind of concerto grosso, and that there is a kind of jazz-singer who is in the tradition of coloratura. Pop singers are in a class of their own.

One more category — pop religious music. It is almost impossible to evaluate it in purely musical or purely religious terms. It has to be thought of in terms of history — the medieval morality plays, the processions of statues of saints in Roman Catholic countries, the playing of brass bands and the banging of tambourines by the Salvation Army, hot-gospelling in American Baptist churches and, in our modern age, the rubbing of gleeful hands in the box office, in the recording studios, and in the offices of the Performing Right Society when Jesus plays to crowded houses. The founder of the Salvation Army saw no reason why the devil should have all the best tunes. He forebade his followers to go to the opera but encouraged them to play operatic overtures on street corners.

Music critics avoid such questions. Let us, however, not avoid music critics.

CHAPTER FOURTEEN

CRITICS

Most of the critics who write for the 'heavies' or who review records on radio are men of learning and experience, deserving a certain respect. They also deserve a degree of scepticism. Again and again you will find that a performer praised in one paper finds little to his satisfaction in another. For this reason beware of saying, after reading one review, 'They didn't think much of him' when the truth is 'He didn't think much of him'.

If you go to a concert and then read a review the next morning you will sometimes wonder whether you and the critic were in the same hall. If the playing was that bad, why did the audience ask for three encores? There is a partial explanation for this. If a critic thinks that the tempo of a slow movement was too fast and says so, he may use up half of his available space. So half of his space is used up to criticise a twentieth of the recital. From a journalistic point of view praise can become boring.

Are artists sensitive to criticism? Yes, particularly in their youth. The beginner on the concert platform feels that one bad notice may ruin the whole of his or her future career. The international star may be too busy catching a plane the next morning even to bother to read the newspaper. Young artists should be warned that they cannot hope to please everyone. In every audience there is someone who refuses to applaud. In my own 'recitalising' I have bowed to an audience clamouring for an encore and spotted, somewhere in Row X, one miserable man whose whole attitude seems to say 'What in Heaven's name are they clapping for?' He follows me around, and perhaps it is just as well that he should. Artists easily succumb to vanity.

Some critics are at their best when not writing 'crits'. In general articles, not written against the clock, they reveal themselves as scholars who, having heard everyone perform everything everywhere, having reviewed many learned tomes, having compared recordings old and new, offer truly interesting reflections on certain musical topics. In common with musicologists at universities, they compel performers to re-think. There will never be amity between artists and critics, but they need one another.

For most critics the writing of newspaper notices is only part of their activities. They pour out histories, biographies and reference books, the best of which are very good and should be collected.

CHAPTER FIFTEEN

BACKGROUND

Listening to music you begin to ask questions. Why are Mahler's symphonies longer than Mozart's? Why do the love songs in operettas go in waltz time? How many meanings attach to the expression 'classical music'? Do visits to composers' birthplaces enhance our understanding of their music?

If you feel you love and understand a great deal of music without studying history or going on long journeys, good luck to you. You are not necessarily inferior to someone who has attended a master class in Salzburg or witnessed a Tchaikovsky ballet in St. Petersburg. (I beg its pardon: Leningrad.) Nevertheless many music lovers do want to know more than the music itself. I would certainly encourage you to read some history and biography. Not all 'Lives of Composers' are interesting, but some are almost incredible. Compare bachelor Brahms with great-lover Liszt and then compare their love songs. You may not come to any conclusions, but there may be value in inconclusive reflections.

If you can manage to hear Wagner at Bayreuth or Verdi at La Scala in Milan you may decide that performances you heard in London or Edinburgh or wherever were better but you will never forget the experience. Wouldn't you like to hear a musical on Broadway itself?

Volumes can be written about background, atmosphere, *ambience*. Here I can allow myself only a few jottings.

In the eighteenth century there began to be a music industry consisting of publishers, instrument makers, performance managers — and critics. In the nineteenth century the aristocratic patron was challenged by the Philharmonic (music loving) Society. Some of these societies founded orchestras: these were the original Philharmonic orchestras. The word is now anyone's to use.

There was a spread of musical education. Napoleon sanctioned the founding of the Conservatoire in Paris. Mendelssohn greatly helped the establishment of the Konservatorium in Leipzig.

In London the Academy and the College were Royal. In New York the National Conservatory was founded by a tycoon's wife. She persuaded Dvořák to be its director. It was during his stay in America that he composed the Symphony called 'From the New World.'

The musical and cultural map seemed to grow larger. Jews emerged from the ghettoes of eastern Europe and became performers, particularly as pianists and violinists. As for composers, both Mendelssohn and Mahler were of Jewish parentage. In due course, the British, importers of music and musicians, began to challenge the foreigners, and now we busily export the music of Elgar, Vaughan Williams, Walton, Britten, Tippett and many others.

The great centres of light music were Vienna, Paris, and London. Then there was Tin Pan Alley, New York.

The effect of music can never be measured. Congreve wrote 'Music hath charms to soothe the savage breast'. What! A war dance? Music can be propaganda, religious or political. It can acquire an aura of culture: Gluck's *Orpheus,* Strauss's *Elektra,* Verdi's *Macbeth.* Observe the well-read composer. Music can be Biblical without being religious — think of Walton's *Belshazzar's Feast.* It can undoubtedly be erotic, but who can possibly censor it? Just where would you cut the Prelude to Wagner's *Tristan and Isolde?* Stage action may be denounced as unacceptable to respectable people, but music itself is always enigmatic.

Although the effect of music cannot be measured, this is not to say that it has no effect. When rock music has run its course there will be musicologists and social historians trying to decide whether it was part of a dangerous drug culture or only the usual act of defiance by young people against parents and teachers. (They have to, don't they? I mean, you know what youngsters are like?)

What of the influence of science? Towards the end of the last century the automatic piano made its appearance. This is usually referred to as the pianola, though Pianola properly belonged to only one make of piano. It was a sort of computer. It was programmed by cutting suitable holes and slots in the moving roll of paper. The paper slid across a long bar pierced by holes. When a slot corresponded with a hole in the bar, the external air rushed through into a vacuum caused by a pump, down a communicating pipe, and into the piano-action. And a note sounded. Later there were improved models that allowed the owner of the piano to make it go louder and softer, or faster and slower, so that he became something like an orchestral conductor. Finally there was the reproducing piano that faithfully performed like a particular famous pianist. Inventors had discovered how to measure the moment when a note began, the moment when it ended, and the velocity of every hammer-stroke, and there were intricate devices to monitor pneumatic pressure accordingly.

Surely this would make most pianists unnecessary? It did not. More dangerous to professional pianists — except a few — was the invention of the gramophone (phonograph). It drove many piano makers into bankruptcy. But in spite of everything the parents of today still send their children to the piano teacher. Myself a pianist, I know I am much envied by non-pianists.

Now we have the synthesiser. Is this a musical instrument? For myself, I have to say that nothing is a musical instrument unless you can sit at it or pick it up and improvise without calculation. For me there has to be a certain kind of intimate bodily contact. How otherwise can there be a flight of fancy?

However, it is with regret that I observe that your composer of today seldom writes piano pieces. Will the pianoforte, like the harpsichord, become a period instrument?

Be sure that in the future the art of music will be influenced by — and at the same time will resist the influence of — the computer, the silicon chip, space travel, and other marvels of science. But no new source of energy can replace that patient and responsive muscle, the human heart.

What of the human mind? As a music lover do you need to be highly educated? Must you be a 'culture vulture'? Does the word 'background' suggest a knowledge of foreign languages and familiarity with all the non-musical arts? There are no easy answers to these questions. We can observe, however, that creativity is in many respects independent of education. It seems that Mozart never went to school. Travelling from court to court when he was an infant prodigy he picked up languages. Working in the opera house he was bound to know the classic legends that were part of a librettist's stock in trade. He knew the requirements of church music. He knew, in fact, what it was necessary for him to know. He was ignorant of earlier music and was well on in his career when his attention was drawn to the music of Bach. Until then, the name Bach had meant Johann Christian Bach whom Mozart as a child had met in London. Johann Sebastian was a revelation. Can we say that Mozart lacked 'background'?

Reflecting on this strange phenomenon we can perhaps say that you too must search for what you need to know. If you have records you will surely need to have, perhaps in paperback, some biographies, some musical histories, a collection of opera stories, perhaps one of the shorter encyclopaedias. In your public library you may find some magazines devoted to music and you may decide to subscribe to one of them. You may look at each week's programmes on Radio Three. You may read record reviews and join one of those clubs that provide you with a choice of records every month. If you live in or near London you will join the throngs at the BBC Promenade Concerts. Making friends with other prom-goers you will probably hear some enthusiastic talk of pieces of music you have never heard.

I would never recommend anyone to write a list of the hundred greatest masterpieces with a view to working through them. One might as well ask for a list of a hundred beautiful women or men and decide to fall in love with each in turn. No: a more natural process is to go, perhaps, to a chamber concert and hear some Haydn, Mozart and Schubert and then to say to yourself 'I've always loved Mozart but tonight I honestly think I enjoyed the Haydn even more. I must *get* some Haydn. I'll look him up in one of those little Master Musicians books and see what's recommended'. Or, again, you may read that not many years ago Sibelius was popular while Mahler was neglected, and you may be moved to have a go at some Sibelius symphonies. And a friend may say 'I'm glad you feel like that: try No. 2'. Falling in love with Puccini's *Manon Lescaut* you may feel a strong desire to compare it with Massenet's *Manon.* Swept off your feet by Rachmaninov's *Rhapsody on a theme of Paganini* you may want to hear Brahms's *Variations on a theme of Paganini* after which you may find yourself irresistably drawn to Paganini's *Caprices* for unaccompanied violin which in turn will lead you to Liszt's transcriptions of Paganini. Follow the trails. Collect opinions and think about them even if they seem a bit wilful. (I happen to think that Chopin is a tougher composer — has more steel in him — than Brahms.) Develop an empathy about other people's beliefs so that you can be a Protestant while listening to the *St. Matthew Passion,* a Roman Catholic during a performance of *The Dream of Gerontius* and a Jew in the presence of Bloch's *Avodath hakodesh* (Sacred Service).

There is a sense in which you must work at music. For an example of evasion of work, just look at one of those electronic organs, sometimes described as fun organs, that are programmed to provide an automatic accompaniment in any standard rhythm and in any key. You press a switch labelled, say, Rumba; up comes the accompaniment; you then play the tune with one finger. Used as a labour saving device, this expensive toy is almost a defence against Beethoven. Used in another way, who knows? A gifted child, starting with it may (though with difficulty) end up as a cathedral organist.

The pursuit of music . . . you will never reach the crock of gold at the end of the rainbow, but you will have the rainbow as company.

What of the questions in the first paragraph of this chapter? Why *are* Mahler's symphonies longer than Mozart's? It was part of the romantic impulse never to say enough is enough, to be ready to die of love, to reach for the heavens. Furthermore in the capital cities of the Romanovs, the Hapsburgs, and the Hohenzollerns (and, formerly, the Bourbons and the Bonapartes) there were big opera houses, big orchestras with technologically improved instruments, and 'big' conductors. And there was big money in London and New York. So why not? After two world wars, heaven-storming romanticism is, for our composers, out. But not for us listeners.

Why *do* love songs in operettas go in waltz time? There is no simple, complete answer. However, say *one two three*. Now say *one and and*. Still better say: *and* ONE *and, and* TWO *and, my* DAR*ling, I* LOVE *you* . . .

Classical music: classical can mean posh music of any era or the music of 'classical proportions' of Haydn and Mozart. The bridge between classical and romantic is Beethoven.

CHAPTER SIXTEEN

BOOKSHELF

A music-lover's collection of books on music should reflect his or her personality and not be tied to a recommended list. We have our special tastes. One collector pursues books with such titles as Great Opera Houses of the World or maybe Passion and Intrigue at La Scala. Another wants a monograph on the medieval motet. Some can never read enough of great pianists, great conductors, great violinists while others subscribe to a society for the preservation of antique instruments.

Some need a pronouncing dictionary and are scrupulous in referring to a sinfoh*neeya* concher*tahn*tay. They talk of a fantai*zeeya* and wonder if there is a difference between *fantastique* and *fantasque.*

Concerning biographies, I would say that the most romantic, almost incredible stories attach themselves to Wagner, Liszt, and Berlioz. Chopin-lovers will go well out of their way to see the house in which Chopin lived with the lady novelist who called herself George Sand. I don't mean that tourist trap Valdemosa in Majorca but, rather, Mme Sand's country house at Nohant, near Chateauroux, south-west of Paris. (She was a great campaigner for women's rights.)

There are books analysing Beethoven's sonatas, psychologising Tchaikovsky's homosexuality, or making a Marxist tract (tract?) out of a Mass by Mozart.

There are books that remind one of the sentence in a little girl's essay on her Christmas present: 'Auntie gave me a book on ponies. This tells me more about ponies than I want to know.'

Is there an irreducible collection? I suggest:
1. *The Oxford Companion to Music* in one plump volume. Much relied on, often quoted, a true companion. There is also a shorter, cheaper version.
2. *A New Dictionary of Music* by Arthur Jacobs (Penguin), a mine of information for quick reference. Inexpensive paperback.
3. *The Master Musicians:* a series of books, each on one composer. As small volumes they only briefly summarise composers' lives, but they include intelligent comment on principal works and are admirably indexed.
4. *The Penguin Book of Lieder:* The German poems and, alongside them, excellent translations. 18 composers represented.
5. *Kobbe's Complete Opera Book* (Putnam) is the big, comprehensive work. An investment. There are smaller, less expensive summaries of libretti, and the principal operas have their stories summarised in the Oxford Companion.
6. *A Short History of Western Music* by Arthur Jacobs (Pelican), packed tight with facts about music, very little about the composers as people.

I am all for buying good books on music, and I must remind anyone who borrows one to return it. How often I have looked for one of my books and discovered that it has gone missing.

You might do worse than look for two books of mine. They are: *Grand Piano*, a history of pianos, pianists, piano-composers, teachers; and *The Young Person's Guide to Playing the Piano* (both Faber & Faber).

GLOSSARY

You buy a recital programme and you see something like this:

Sonata quasi una fantasia, in C-sharp minor, Op. 27 No. 2   BEETHOVEN
('Moonlight Sonata')
Adagio sostenuto
Allegretto
Presto agitato

Some of these Italian terms may be familiar to you. Others can be looked up in the sort of pocket dictionary that every music lover has somewhere on his bookshelves. Beware, however! Dictionary definitions can be misleading or puzzling. *Sostenuto* means sustained: how does a performer sustain music? *Staccato* means detached: how does one detach a note? There is no need to know all possible words in Italian, German and French, but the most-used Italian expressions may be worth attention.

Tempo

Prestissimo: top speed.

Presto: really fast. A baroque presto probably not as fast as a romantic presto.

Allegro: originally merry. In musicians' Italian it means fast.

Allegretto: somewhat allegro, often associated with some such word as *grazioso* (grahtzió zo), graceful.

Moderato (modderah' toh): cannot be fixed as a metronome speed. It is the tempo that seems neither fast nor slow in relation to a particular piece.

Andante (andan'tay): going along. In musicians' Italian it means a leisurely tempo, not obviously slow.

Andantino (andanteé no): somewhat andante (whatever that may mean).

Adagio (adah' zho) slow.

Lento: slow.

Largo: large, broad, dignified.

Observe *molto* and *assai* (a-sigh) meaning very. Thus allegro molto or allegro assai mean much the same as presto.

Accelerando (ak-chel-er-and' oh): accelerating.

Rallentando:
Ritardando: slowing. These words can imply different degrees of gradualness.

Più mosso and *meno mosso*: more moved and less moved — not gradually but immediately faster or slower.

Tempo primo: after various changes of tempo this is an instruction to return to the first tempo of the movement.

* The stressed syllable is underlined

Loudness

ff	*fortissimo*	very loud
f	*forte*	loud
mf	*mezzo forte*	medium loud (*mezzo* is pronounced metź-oh).
mp	*mezzo piano*	medium soft
p	*piano*	soft
pp	*pianissimo*	very soft

(most of these words are adjectives not adverbs: forte is loud, not loudly).

Just as there is no absolute speed for moderato, there is no absolute standard of loudness. The fortissimo of a string quartet is not that of a brass band, but it may be just as exciting. In relation to softness it is worth mentioning once more that intimate softness is not the same as loudness in the distance though both may be marked *pp* .

Crescendo (cresheń do): gradually increasing the tone. ◁————— is the sign for the word. The journalistic expression 'rising to a crescendo' is nonsense. A crescendo may begin as *pp* and arrive at *mp* . A crescendo is not necessarily perfectly graded. Imagine yourself saying (crescendo): louder and *loude*r and LOUDer. 'The ers' and the 'ands' remains soft, but the general effect is crescendo. Some *crescendi* rise vigorously: others very gradually.

Diminuendo: this word is more frequent than the equivalent decrescendo. ————▷ is the sign. The opposite of crescendo. Interestingly, a long and gradual *dim.* is much rarer than a long, gradual *cresc.* However, the end of a romantic piece may be marked *morendo* — dying away.

Poco a poco: little by little.

Subito (soo' betoh): suddenly, immediately.

Marcato (marcáh toe): marked, accented.

Pesante (pesáhn te): heavily.

Martellato (martelláh toe): hammered (rarely seen but important, applying to piano music).

Sforzando (sfortzán doh): forcing the tone, a fierce accent (in relation to the context).

Quasi (kwah'-zee): almost, as if, in the manner of . . .

Character

Con brio (breé oh): Brio is the quality one expects from a tenor at a moment of operatic heroism. In instrumental music it is 'manly' vigour.

Dolce (dol' che): sweetly, with 'feminine' gentleness. (Music is a sexist art. A woman pianist must be able to play music composed by men to be played on an instrument designed for a man's hand. Conversely a man must be able to 'nurse' the instrument.)

Con fuoco: with fire.

Vivace (vevah' che): vivacious, full of life.

Cantabile (cantah' belay): in a singing style. This applies particularly and frequently to piano music. In cold fact every piano note begins with a bump of sound and then decays. However, an illusion of singing tone can be produced (preferably on an expensive instrument) if notes other than the melody are soft and if the melody-notes are variably loud to suggest the accents of poetry. In a Nocturne marked *pp* the melody may, in fact, be pretty loud while conveying an impression of warmth and 'roundness'. Cantabile is usually associated with legato.

Legato (legah' toh): bound together, smooth. Each note is heard right up to the moment when the next begins. However, there may be a tiny silence before a new phrase to suggest the taking of a breath.

Staccato (stacah' toh): detached. Think of playing a scale on the piano with one finger, hopping from note to note.

Pizzicato (pitzycah' toh): a string player's word: plucking the strings instead of bowing them. A ping-ping-ping effect.

Sostenuto (sostenoó toh): every note well held, scrupulously legato. Brahms uses the word to suggest a slow tempo.

Other words

Suite: a set of pieces, not as unified as a sonata. Often there is an over-all title plus separate titles. In the baroque era there were dance-suites (sarabande, gavotte, gigue, etc.). Sometimes a suite consists of excerpts from 'incidental' music.

Incidental Music: music in the theatre, not for an opera but for a play. A well known example is Grieg's music for Ibsen's *Peer Gynt.* Sometimes incidental music is in contrast to the mood of the characters. A lively dance, the 'farandole', in Bizet's The Maid of Arles *(L'Arlésienne)* is the background to a tragedy.

Programme Music: such as 'Wellington's Victory' (the *Battle Symphony*) by Beethoven; *1812* by Tchaikovsky; '*The Sorceror's Apprentice*' by Dukas; '*Night on the Bare Mountain*' by Mussorgsky.

Variations: as variation succeeds variation, the theme is more and more disguised: e.g. a major tune becomes minor, a fast tempo is changed into that of a funeral march, a solemn tune reappears as a dance, a treble tune is just discernible in the bass or in an inner part, etc. Often the theme is borrowed — Variations on a theme by . . . In the *'Enigma' Variations* Elgar's theme was inspired by a tune that the composer never divulged. Each variation is a musical portrait of one of his friends.

Continuo: in the baroque era musicians were expected to be skilled at improvising. Sometimes a composer would write a bass line, to be played maybe on a cello; above this a harpsichordist would improvise a complete accompaniment. Occasionally, under the bass-line, the composer would write figures — a shorthand indication of suitable chords. Hence the expression 'figured bass'.

Ornaments ('Grace Notes'): it was a sign of good taste in a performance in the eighteenth century for a singer or player to embellish a melody with shivers and shakes and trills and turns, not necessarily in obedience to established rules. If a listener of that era could hear a modern performance he might exclaim, 'But they have no taste!'

Transcription: in such a piece the notes are by no means trans-scribed: they are freely arranged and re-arranged, often to make a brilliant effect. Curiously, a more respectful kind of copying is called an arrangement — for example a song arranged as violin solo, where the violinist plays pretty much what a singer would sing. Concertos are usually published with the solo part plus 'reduction' for piano — a useful arrangement of the orchestral score for the purpose of rehearsal.

Signatures: 1) A key signature is a cluster of sharps or flats at the beginning of a line of music. For example, 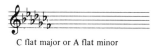 tells the performer to play every F or C or G as a sharp unless one of those notes is preceded by a 'natural' sign. Three sharps indicate A-major or F-sharp minor. Every major key has its relative minor. The maximum number of sharps or flats in a key signature is seven.

C flat major or A flat minor

2) A time signature indicates the number of beats in a bar and the value of each. So $\frac{3}{4}$ indicates three quarter-notes (crotchets).

① ② ③

Though five, seven, and other figures may indicate unusual numbers of beats the customary numbers are 2, 3, or 4 in 'simple time'. If the upper number is 6, 9 or 12 we are in the realm of 'compound time' and the beats can be counted in two ways. In slow tempo a conductor would conduct in six: in fast tempo in two.

Drink to me on-ly with thine eyes, And
1 2 3 4 5 6 1 2 3 4 5 6
or 1   2   1   2

Since you are likely to read a book on music written by an American author, you may like to know that Americans, like Germans, regard 𝅝 as the whole note — the longest in general use — and then talk of half-notes, quarter-notes etc. In Britain the whole-note is called semibreve. On the face of it, this word means half-short and is a quaint hangover from medieval notation. Our next longest note is equally strangely called minim, and we continue with the crotchet, the quaver, the semiquaver etc. By the way, the French *croche* does not mean crotchet: it means quaver.

In America the upright stroke before each regular down-beat is called bar, not barline, and the duration from one such to another is not bar but measure. On one side of the Atlantic six quavers in a bar: on the other six eighth-notes in a measure.

Phrase: there is no exact definition for this, but you will understand what a singing-teacher means by 'Take a breath before each phrase.' Since music is largely a song-and-dance act it is necessary for string players and pianists to learn how to make the music breathe. Phrasing is intimately involved with accentuation not necessarily indicated by accent-signs. The length of a phrase only rarely corresponds with the length of a bar. Sometimes the length of a phrase is indicated by a curved line called a slur, but slurs have other meanings too, and can indicate how many notes are to be played during a down- or up-bow in string-music.

Hark, hark! the lark at Heavn's gate sings, And Phoe-bus 'gins_ to rise_____ His

Initials: Mozart's works, lacking opus numbers, were catalogued by Ludwig von Köchel. Hence Concerto in A, K488. Since then other catalogues have been compiled. Schubert's works are D-numbered by Otto Deutsch; Haydn's are Hob-numbered by Anthony von Hoboken; and Bach's are BWV-numbered in the *Bach Werke Verzeichnis* compiled by Wolfgang Schmieder.

Canon (Canonic Imitation): think of a children's 'round'. The girls begin a tune; one bar later the boys begin the same tune; it all fits together. This is the simplest kind of canon. The most complex could consist of a tune going forwards being accompanied by the same tune going backwards. And there are other ingenuities.

Cadenza: in early concertos the word was printed, the music being improvised (?) by the soloist, the orchestra falling silent. Nineteenth century concertos usually included composed cadenzas in a quasi-improvisatory style. Some pianists have published cadenzas suitable for concertos that lack them. Hummel, a pupil of Mozart, did this effectively. In many of Liszt's solo pieces there are, from time to time, cascades of notes, pianistic fireworks that also are called cadenzas. There are two in *Liebestraum*. (There are three pieces with this title: one is the Dream of Love we all love.)

Listener's Notes

Title / Composer

Performance details

Comments

Listener's Notes

Title / Composer

Performance details

Comments